CONNECTING THE DOTS

*My Life and Inventions,
From X-rays to Death Rays*

Robert Howard

WELCOME RAIN PUBLISHERS, LLC
NEW YORK

To Kit

CONTENTS

Preface

CHANCES ARE, YOU DON'T KNOW ME. I've never been a very public person. You won't find 1,346,522 references to me in a search on the Internet; in fact, unless you work at it, you may not even find one. But I am not Robert E. Howard, the writer of fantasy pulp stories and creator of Conan the Barbarian. I am not pro-wrestler Bob "Hardcore" Holly, whose real name was Robert Howard. I am not Robert Howard, the famous American triple jumper. And I am not any of the Bob Howards who own car dealerships in what seems to be every state in the union.

I am the Robert Howard whose career led to many of the inventions that play a part, both large and small, in many of the things you probably take for granted every day:

- Try to imagine life without a rectangular TV picture tube. That's right, there was a time, about sixty years ago, when all picture tubes were round. My television company accelerated the development of an affordable rectangular picture tube at the start of the television age.
- I also helped invent the cable TV system, which for the first time brought many channels into homes with television sets that could not receive clear, ghost-free, over-the-air broadcasts.
- Thanks to one of my inventions, all X-rays taken today are sharper and easier for radiologists to read in order to make a diagnosis.

- If you had a printer hooked up to your computer in the 1980s and early 1990s, chances are it was a dot matrix printer. That was my invention, too. Almost all the desktop laser printers today are based on the use of semiconductor lasers and electronics that were also my joint inventions, just as most of today's ink-jet printers are based on one of my patents, which uses piezoelectric crystals to spit out tiny dots of ink onto a piece of paper.

- There was a time when computers could not "talk" directly to printers and other peripherals without a unique connector. I co-invented the first universally adopted computer interface, called the Centronics interface, which was faster, cost less, and was more reliable than any other interface in use at that time. It remained the standard until the USB interface we use today took its place in the late 1990s.

- My inventions also led to improvements in the quality of phonograph records and the quality of professionally printed color photographs, while lowering their cost. The former are now obsolete; the latter may soon be.

- I was responsible for creating a computerized "cash register" system to prevent illegal skimming in casino operations; I also developed an electronic slot machine, which allows payoffs much greater than any mechanical slot machine ever could.

- My inventions moved the offset color printing industry into the new world of digital printing technology. This led to the creation of the short-run color printing business, which accounts for 80 percent of all professional color printing jobs today.

- Last, and maybe not least, I helped develop a new offensive laser weapon for the military, as well as a new defensive technology that can neutralize roadside bombs.

The book you hold in your hands is the story of those inventions and of my life. I began writing it in late 2001 in the newly decorated study of my villa on a small peninsula in southern France. From where I sat I could look out at the blue Mediterranean as it slapped up against the beach, the skyline of Nice in the distance. We purchased this magnificent villa in 1989. The other half of this "we" is Kit Smith, my third wife and soul mate, whom I am fortunate to have met at this stage in my life. We were married in 1987 after a courtship of two years. We have loved and enjoyed most of the same things in life, and now, after more than two decades, we still do.

Probably no one in the Brooklyn of my youth, where I grew up and went to school, had ever heard of Cap Ferrat, which was once the domain of King Leopold II of Belgium. But this little strip of land on the French Riviera is where I finally found some peace and tranquility in my twilight years, at least until 2006, when I sold the villa because of changed world conditions and post-9/11 travel requirements. That's when I started my twenty-eighth company, Ionatron, Inc., now named Applied Energetics, in Tucson, Arizona. But I'm getting ahead of myself.

All my life, or at least for the past sixty years or so, I was a high-pressure businessman with a type A personality. Now, at the age of eighty-five and before it gets too late, I have the time and a burning desire to tell the story of my life, my inventions, my entrepreneurial accomplishments, my failures, my friends, and my family of five children and twelve grandchildren, as well as the large number of other people who have come to be dependent on me emotionally, financially, or both.

Of course, I am proud of my many accomplishments, including:

- my dozens of state-of-the art inventions

- the twenty-nine successful companies I started or acquired
- the billions of dollars that I created for my shareholders
- the tens of millions of dollars I have given to numerous charities
- the tens of thousands of jobs my businesses have created
- the new industries created by my inventions
- the hundreds of lives that I have helped personally
- and the family of five children and twelve grandchildren whom I love dearly

But my proudest accomplishment and greatest pleasure is knowing every day that I have improved the quality of the lives of a large number of people—family and friends, of course, but many others as well. This derives from a simple philosophy, "the joy of giving," that my loving grandfather, Isaac Greenspoon, ingrained in me all those years ago. Isaac, who was my mother's father, was my mentor. Though he died in 1938, he lives on in my mind every day.

•••1•••

Top Drawer Kid

For me, it all started on the kitchen table on the fourth floor of a walk-up apartment building on Howard Avenue in the Brownsville section of Brooklyn. On May 19, 1923, a premature, three-pound nine-ounce baby boy was born, yes, on the kitchen table, to Gertrude (née Greenspoon) and Samuel Horowitz. I was their second child, born nearly four years after my sister, Sylvia, and named Robert Emanuel.

My loving parents: Samuel and Gertrude Horowitz (1918)

1

The world I was born into would seem unbelievably primitive today. In 1923, there were almost no telephones and no televisions or computers. The world's first domestic refrigerator was sold in Sweden that year. The 19th Amendment to the Constitution had given women the right to vote throughout the United States just three years earlier, the same year as the world's first licensed radio broadcast. And a Spanish inventor designed the autogiro, the precursor of the modern helicopter in 1923. That was also the year that Yankee Stadium opened in the Bronx for its first baseball game and Edwin Hubble gave us the first scientific estimate of the size of the universe. I would have a not insignificant impact on the technological innovations of the remainder of the century, but first I had to make my way out of the drawer.

Since I was born almost three months premature, my parents had hastily prepared my first "crib," the top drawer of the dresser in their bedroom. From that time in the drawer until the age of twenty-one, when my sister married a radiologist named Murray Fuhrman and I inherited her bedroom with an adjoining bath, I never had my own room. My bedroom was the dining room of each apartment we lived in, and we lived in dozens of different rental apartments over those two decades. I slept on a fold-up bed, which was stored in a closet during the day and taken out each night after everyone else went to bed.

When I was about three years old, we moved to the Brighton Beach section of Coney Island in Brooklyn. My father worked the midnight to 8 a.m. shift for the United States Post Office Central Branch at Penn Station in midtown Manhattan. His job as a timekeeper for the U.S. Post Office was the most desirable and secure position to have during the Great Depression. Of course, like most other government employees at that time, he was forced to take a 10 percent salary cut for three years, but

The future
entrepreneur and
inventor at the age
of two and a half

at least he had a steady job, received a paycheck every week, and put food on the table for the family. What it meant to grow up during the Depression is something that today's children would have great difficulty understanding.

Being a timekeeper was the only position my father held throughout his life, other than the moonlighting job he held as a ticket collector at Ebbets Field, where the Brooklyn Dodgers played. During the day, he went to the beach, played handball, or wrestled. He was also a charter member of the Coney Island Polar Bear Club, which meant that he would swim in the Atlantic Ocean on the coldest days of the winter, regardless of any snow and ice, wearing only an ordinary bathing suit.

We had a lot of fun together at the beach. Embroidered on the front of my handmade bathing suit were the words MY BOY. That's who I was—His Boy. My sister also loved the beach, not for the water so much as for the punching bags available in an open-air building on the beach. The building had a flat ceiling with dozens of metal plates into which were screwed the punching bags. The beach supplied numerous small wooden platforms around the floor to raise you to the height necessary to have the bag about even with your face in order to punch it properly. Since I was less than four years old, we had to stack up at least three or four platforms so that I could reach the bag.

As the years passed, I grew larger and stronger than my sister, though it really bothered me that she was better than me at everything. The fact that she was a lot smarter, thinner, faster, and prettier made her everyone's favorite, including my mother and father, though my sister claims otherwise. The only exception I am certain of was my grandfather, Isaac Greenspoon, who absolutely adored me. When I was six years old, my grandmother was killed when a taxi backed up and crushed her. This left a gaping hole in my grandfather's life and, fortunately, he looked to me to fill that void. To this day I have countless pleasant memories of the things that he taught me during the times we spent together alone.

Grandfather Isaac was a wonderful and most unusual man. In 1910, he left behind a wife and three children in Odessa, Russia, to immigrate to America. To provide for his passage and acquire the income he needed to sustain his wife and three

Father and son in 1931: Dad always referred to me as "My Boy."

children in Russia while he established himself in the New World, he sold his window-shade business in Odessa for some cash up-front and additional funds to be a paid over a four-year period. Isaac's brother, who had gone to America three years earlier and was already in the process of bringing his family over, helped him get established in the New World. The business expertise Isaac had gained in Russia allowed him to launch a successful business in New York City very quickly. He had had the foresight to send ahead to his brother a large amount of raw material plus some finished, standard-size window shades. Soon after his arrival he was selling window shades from a pushcart on the Lower East Side.

Isaac Greenspoon was my grandfather and my inspiration.

Isaac would cut and assemble his window shades in the basement of the tenement rooming house where he rented a room, and the next day he would deliver the previous day's orders. Working day and night, he was able to raise enough money to bring his wife and children, one or two at a time, to

America and provide them with a nice apartment in New York City. The last member of his family joined him about two years after his arrival. You can't help but love, respect, and admire a man who executed this remarkable plan for coming to America with such strength of character and commitment. I am fortunate to have inherited some of that drive and perseverance.

Several years later my grandfather's business was operating from a modest loft in the Brownsville section of Brooklyn, where he installed the most up-to-date machine to produce window shades in an efficient and cost-effective way. Sometimes on Saturdays, I would go into his factory and help out by cleaning up and packing the finished window shades. Once my grandfather allowed me to operate his one cherished machine. The procedure involved first adjusting the controls to set the width and length of shade desired. The operator would then take the end of the window shade material and staple it onto a wooden roller, which had a spring inside and pins on each end. Several staples were required to attach the end of the shade to the wooden roller. The operator applied these with a staple gun that was not only shaped like a hammer but also swung as if you were driving in a nail, thereby forcing the staples through the window shade material and into the wooden roller.

In my one and only attempt at making window shades, I very carefully took the end of the window shade, held it in place, and spaced out the staples uniformly. Next, I carefully rolled the shade onto the roller, slipped a piece of wood into a slot at the other end, and put a little string though the hole in the center of the wood. Then I carefully placed the finished shade into a shipping box.

After watching me work for about an hour, my grandfather came to me and said, "Bobby, if you were the operator of this machine, I would be bankrupt in about one month." He explained that because of the high cost of the machine, not to mention the cost of labor and the materials involved, many window shades needed to be produced each hour in order to have a viable business. He then said, "I will operate this machine and show you how I can produce three times as many window shades per hour as you." And indeed he did everything very fast, including hammering the staples so quickly that I could hardly see the hammer moving. When he finished, I took one of his window shades and unwound it, and said, "Your five staples are not evenly spaced—two of them are crooked, and one is not all the way in. The knot on the string on the hole is not tightened all the way."

I've never forgotten his reply. "Bobby," he said, "good engineering is knowing when to draw the line as 'good enough,' because in business, in order to survive and be competitive, you must sell at a price customers will buy from you, and not from your competitor." That was the first rule of business I ever learned.

The fact that my grandfather managed to keep his window shade business going during the Great Depression was a credit to his business skills. The Depression had a devastating impact on everyone, but particularly on those, like my grandfather, who owned a small business. With the construction of new apartments and homes almost at a standstill, the market for new window shades was almost nonexistent. But he was aware that a new innovative window covering called venetian blinds, which came in numerous colors and finishes, seemed to be all the rage at the high end of the meager new construction market. These venetian blinds were selling because their easy and convenient light controls and choice of styles appealed to those who could afford to spend a little more for a window covering.

Isaac's ability to recognize this emerging market was the secret of his success. He quickly purchased the necessary machines and materials to manufacture venetian blinds efficiently, and he directed his advertising at those who could afford a more expensive window shade. Over time I came to understand that this is what enabled my grandfather to do well in business. He was wise and insightful, and business came naturally to him. I was the apple of my grandfather's eye and he was my teacher. He played an incredibly important part in my development as a youngster.

Each winter, for several years, we would go by train for long weekends and holidays to Lakewood, New Jersey, where he owned a small house in the country. At that time Lakewood was a winter and summer resort, mostly for affluent people from New York City. The love and camaraderie that my grandfather and I developed during this period created an everlasting bond between us. In the winter, we would take leisurely rides on the snow-covered roads in a horse-drawn sled. It was so thrilling for me to be able to hold the reins of the horse and snap the whip to make the horses go faster! It was also in Lakewood that I first learned to ice-skate, a sport which became a major asset during my adolescent years. My grandfather bought me my first, second, and third pairs of ice skates to keep up with my very rapid growth during those years.

At home, when the pond in the nearby park was frozen over, I was out skating every chance I could. Then, when I was about eight years old, we moved from Brighton Beach to the Flatbush section of Brooklyn, which, fortunately for me, was not only very close to my grandfather's home, but also to Ebbets Field, and about two miles from the Brooklyn Ice Palace. The Rogers Avenue trolley line ran directly in front our house and stopped within a hundred yards of the ice rink. Since I couldn't afford the nickel fare, I would grab onto the steel bars on the rear window and stand on the cowcatcher, out of the view of the conductor. (There was a cowcatcher at both ends of the trolley, so that when the motorman reached the of the line, he would simply move to the back of the car, activate the controls there, and drive in the opposite direction.) The cowcatcher, which prevented anything from going under the car, gave me a nice platform to stand on and provided free transportation to and from the Brooklyn Ice Palace, about a three-minute trip each way.

The next hurdle was the cost of admission. Since I was a likable, chubby little kid with considerable skills in charming people, I was able to befriend the older man who was in charge of caring for the rink and cleaning the ice every hour or two. Between public sessions and hockey practices, I would wiggle my way into the arena and help the crew clean the ice. This allowed me to skate during the public sessions without paying. And because I went out on the ice with a hockey stick and a T-shirt I had purchased from one the instructors at the ice rink, I looked official enough for the coaches of the various hockey teams that played there to ask for my assistance on occasion.

The skills I acquired on skates and playing ice hockey would later enable me to attend the high school of my choice and receive a scholarship to Columbia University, a pair of achievements that would have been otherwise impossible, as my grades were barely passing. Though I didn't know it at the time, I suffered from a learning handicap known as dyslexia, which makes reading and spelling difficult. To top it off, I was also often in trouble growing up—with just about everyone, including my sister, Sylvia.

There were times when Sylvia and I didn't even talk to each other. I remember one time in particular. Sylvia was majoring in art at the best high school for the arts in New York City, Girls Commercial High School in the Prospect Park section of Brooklyn. For homework, the students were required to make watercolor paintings of scenery, fruit bowls, and, luckily for me, nude models. Occasionally, my sister would come home with two or three of her friends, and in her room, behind a closed door, they would take turns posing nude for one another. Over the door of her room was a transom that was always kept open for ventilation. Just outside was a sewing machine with a chair, so it was a simple thing to climb very quietly from the chair onto the sewing machine (with a telephone book on top for the

Beautiful at any age: my sister, Sylvia Fuhrman, in a glamour pose

smaller kids) and peer through the transom at the naked girl on the other side.

One of the most beautiful girls among my sister's friends was Edythe Marrener. She would pose from time to time and later became the very successful, Academy Award–winning actress named Susan Hayward. When she would pose nude, I would charge my friends ten cents instead of the five cents I charged for viewing the other girls.

Thus, my skills as an entrepreneur became apparent at an early age.

One day every week, I would charge my friends for one minute of peeking, until the time a big fat kid slipped and fell as he got down from the sewing machine. My sister quickly opened the door and saw what was going on. She said that for doing that to her she would never speak to me again. She told my mother, who immediately moved the sewing machine and chair away from the door. That was the end of my first, very profitable business.

I got my first real job when the owner of the local fruit store that my mother frequented hired me to deliver orders of fruit and vegetables to his customers in the neighborhood. I would make the deliveries after school using my new Rollfast bicycle. I loved cherries then, and still do today, so when there were cherries in the package to deliver I would eat a few. Sometimes I might eat more than a few.

One hot summer's day about a year after I started the job, I was given a large bag of cherries on the top of a package, which was the last of three orders to be delivered. The temptation was too much and I ate several cherries between each delivery. When I entered the apartment to make my last delivery, my boss was standing there waiting for me, holding a large scale over his head. He reached into the large bag I was holding, grabbed the now half-empty bag of cherries, put them on the scale, and saw that nearly a half pound of cherries was missing. He then reached into his apron pocket, smashed a very ripe tomato on my forehead, and shouted, "You're fired!" This was the first and last time I was ever fired from a job.

··2··

Breasts, Balls, and Pucks

I WAS A JOCK IN SCHOOL and popular with the girls. I attended Public School 161, located on Crown Street near Nostrand Avenue in the Flatbush section of Brooklyn. At that time, we lived a few blocks away on Montgomery Street near Rogers Avenue in a lovely apartment on the third floor of a four-story walk-up. It had three bedrooms, one for my parents, one for my sister, and one for my Uncle Charley. Many years later I found out that Uncle Charley was not my uncle, but just a boarder who lived with us for many years.

I have memories of several people from P.S. 161, two of whom had a lasting impact on my life. One was Miss Ott, a thin, fairly attractive, but very well-endowed middle-aged music teacher. She dressed in such a way as to show off her out-standing figure, and a number of other boys and I would go out of our way to study music and attend her classes for this reason. Thanks to Miss Ott, I have remained a devotee of this part of the female anatomy all my life. Somewhat less memorable, but more influential, was Mr. Frank, the shop teacher, who gave me extra instruction on using all the different machines and let me use the machine shop to make things in my spare time.

But ice hockey was still my number one passion at the time. In the 1930s, there were two National Hockey League teams in

New York. One was the New York Rangers, the other was the New York Americans. Because there were so few ice-skating rinks in Manhattan, the Americans used the Brooklyn Ice Palace for their practice sessions. I often stayed for these sessions, and after making myself useful for a season, I was offered the job as the team's "stick boy for practices" when the previous stick boy had to resign because his parents were moving out to Long Island. So at the age of ten, I became the stick boy for the New York Americans of the National Hockey League. By listening to the coaches, and playing with anyone who played or practiced at the Brooklyn Ice Palace, I gradually became an excellent hockey player.

As the stick boy for the New York Americans, I also had a free pass to attend their games at Madison Square Garden. Sometimes I would even fill in for the game stick boy, who was much older and able to travel with the team. Once I was asked to be the game stick boy for a Sunday afternoon game in Philadelphia. We had to take a bus and sleep over in Philadelphia on Saturday night so the team could have a practice early Sunday morning. When we arrived, we checked into the hotel and went to our rooms. My room was the clubroom the team used as their meeting room; it had a convertible couch for me to sleep on. The players asked me to stay in the room while they went out for dinner; they promised to send dinner up for me. Just as they were leaving, a good-looking woman of about twenty-five years of age showed up. I heard that she was an exotic dancer who would perform at the after-dinner bachelor party to celebrate the engagement of one of the players.

The woman went into the bathroom to change her clothes and then practiced her performance in the connecting bedroom while she waited for the players to return. I was sitting on the couch listening to the radio, when I heard music from the adjoining room. The connecting door was not closed all the way, so I was able to see into her room. She had a phonograph playing music for her dance routine, which involved slowly removing one piece of clothing after another in time with the music. I was about twelve years old at the time and was very aroused by her dancing and her naked body. At one point, she danced toward the door, swung it open with one hand, and reached in and grabbed my arm. As I stood there looking at her naked body, I had my first unbelievable orgasm. I was not allowed to attend the party that night, but I could not sleep after that experience. The next day on the bus, as I closed my eyes to try to catch up on my sleep, I overheard the players' chatter and learned that her "rehearsal" had been set up for my benefit.

Ice hockey was not my only passion, however. While we lived in Crown Heights and Flatbush, I also followed the Brooklyn Dodgers. They played at nearby Ebbets Field, where my father was a ticket collector. When there was a home game, my father would tell me what gate he would be working at and give me two or three small pieces of colored paper the same color and size as the tickets for that day. I would go to his gate with a friend or two and we would give my father the colored slips of paper as though they were tickets. He would then step on a treadle that released the turnstile and allowed us through the gate and into the ballpark. We would then work our way closer and closer to the field into the reserved section, which usually had many empty seats. With a hot dog and some hot peanuts, we could sit back and really enjoy the games, some of which became quite famous for outstanding plays by their best players. Even then I had entrepreneurial instincts: I would charge everyone except my best friend twenty-five cents to get in to see the Dodgers' games.

A friend of mine at P.S. 161 whose name was Irwin Spitzer always had a baseball and baseball glove with him. Since he wanted to become a pitcher and I was big and strong, I became his catcher. We were inseparable and at every opportunity, he would have me catch for him. The problem was that I had no catcher's mitt, only a regular fielder's glove, so my left hand would always hurt. I asked my father for a catcher's mitt for my birthday, and on that day I received a new mitt. In the box was a first baseman's mitt, however, and a large sponge to be used as a cushion inside the glove. My father explained that a catcher's mitt was too expensive, and besides, the salesman had told him that a lot of catchers used a first baseman's glove. If you believed that, you would believe anything. But I suppose the difference in price made the story believable for my father, since this was, after all, during the height of the Depression.

Shortly after my birthday my father realized how important a catcher's mitt was to me, and he managed to talk the salesman into exchanging the first baseman's glove for a catcher's mitt for a bit more than the price originally quoted for it. P.S. 161 had a baseball team, so naturally Irwin Spitzer became their pitcher and I was their catcher. The second and last season we played together our school almost won the championship. We lost in extra innings, at the bottom of the eleventh, when the first man up on the opposing team hit a home run, ending the game and with it our season.

Irwin and I graduated from P.S. 161 that spring and we both went on to Erasmus Hall High School in Brooklyn. I had really wanted to go to Brooklyn Technical High School, otherwise known as Brooklyn Tech, but my marginal grades made it impossible. Erasmus Hall had an extensive sports program, and Irwin and I both tried out for, and made, the freshman baseball team. Erasmus also had an ice hockey team, but it was not open to freshman. So when the tryouts for the team took place at my home away from home, the Brooklyn Ice Palace, I didn't tell the coach that I was a freshman. I was handed a uniform and quickly went out on the ice just like all the other new kids. After watching us all skate for only a few minutes, the coach singled me out, and I became the best hockey player at Erasmus.

That fall, the Erasmus ice hockey team had a preseason practice game with Brooklyn Tech. We won 5 to 1, and even though I was playing defense, I scored four of our five goals. After the practice, the players all left for the locker rooms, but I stayed to help clean the surface of the ice. That's when the Brooklyn Tech coach called me to the side and asked me if I was Canadian. I told him of my experience at the Brooklyn Ice Palace, and also made it a point to tell him how badly I had wanted to go to Brooklyn Tech but couldn't because of my grades. He asked if I would come to his office at Brooklyn Tech at 9 a.m. the next day, a Saturday morning.

Of course, I was outside his office waiting for him at 8:30. I sat there looking at my watch, and finally at 8:52, he walked in with another gentleman. The two of them asked me dozens of questions in the hour that followed, at the end of which they told me to return as usual to my classes at Erasmus on Monday morning. There was no way I could have predicted what would happen after that meeting, but at about two in the afternoon on Monday I was called in to the principal's office over the public address system. I walked into the principal's office as slowly as I could, fearing the worst; I thought I was in all kinds of trouble for having gone to meet the Brooklyn Tech coach.

Much to my surprise, though, in the principal's office with the Brooklyn Tech coach was a gentleman who introduced himself as George Cummings. He was the assistant principal at

Brooklyn Tech. He said that if I could focus on my grades and do better than I had in the past, I could be admitted to Brooklyn Tech. It was as though the weight of the world had come off my shoulders. It was one of the rare times in my life that left me speechless. After a few moments, with a big smile on my face, I said I would focus every ounce of energy in my body on getting better grades. I was then given a piece of paper for my parents to sign, and the principal told me to empty my locker, take my books with me, and report to Brooklyn Tech the next day. From that day on, I was a student at Brooklyn Tech and played for their ice hockey team.

That ended my baseball ambitions and, for the most part, my very close relationship with Irwin Spitzer, who followed a career in baseball as "Ernie" Spitzer until he was injured in a preseason game while playing for the New York Yankees. Everyone lost track of him at that point. But twenty years later, as I waited for a security gate of a housing project in downtown Brooklyn to open, I noticed to my right a hot dog and Italian food cart with an umbrella. The man running it looked very familiar and wore a New York Yankees baseball cap. I asked his name, and he replied, "Ernie Spitzer." My eyes lit up, and I shouted, "Irwin Spitzer!" I jumped out of the car and we hugged each other, tears filling our eyes. We spent the rest of the afternoon catching up; it was one of the most enjoyable afternoons of my life.

Although Brooklyn Tech was an all-boys school, we had a sister all-girls school, Girls Commercial High School, nearby. They supported us in all sorts of coed activities and supplied cheerleaders for all our teams as though we were a coed school. As a star ice hockey player, I had my pick of the crop; that's when the girls gave me the nickname of "Fingers." The guys called me "Whitey."

• • •

WHEN WORLD WAR II STARTED in Europe, we were living on Beekman Place in Flatbush. Most of my friends were older, so they had to register for the draft. I was only sixteen in 1939 but tall and husky, so I could easily make friends with the older kids. It helped that in early 1940, I bought my first car, a 1932 Pierce-Arrow convertible, which was selling for $25. Actually, I bought it with nine of my friends, so it was my first one-ninth share of a car, but all we could come up with together was $23. So we bought the car without the battery for two dollars less. We had to push the car to get it started. Since this car was such a gas-guzzler, getting only five miles to the gallon, and gasoline was being rationed at the time, every night we had to siphon gasoline from other cars parked on the street. I always had a hard time getting the taste of gasoline out of my mouth afterward.

Having the use of a beautiful and comfortable Pierce-Arrow was a boon to having relationships with cute girls. Mirabelle Elswick was the apple of my eye at the time; she was a gorgeous, sixteen-year-old Southern beauty, and new to New York. Soon after I started to date her—going to movies, having a Coke, taking walks in nearby Prospect Park, and exploring my favorite part of the female anatomy—I learned that she was very popular with some other guys as well. She was easy for them— not me.

Mahland Cann was my best friend at the time. He was as Irish as Irish can be and we were like brothers. Mahland had a job delivering newspapers from the back of a delivery van. In those days, the *Daily News* and the *Daily Mirror* each sold for two cents apiece. The papers printed an edition that came out at 8 p.m. Each evening, people stood on street corners waiting for the newspapers to arrive; it was a citywide ritual. The five or six daytime newspapers published editions throughout the day as well. They were delivered in a small truck with a tailgate and a bar across the back for the thrower to hold on to. So Mahland would stand on the rear platform, hold onto the bar with one hand, and throw out a bundle of newspapers with the other as the truck passed each newsstand.

I sometimes would tag along to help. Sitting inside the truck, I would prepare the next bundle of papers by tying a string around the roll and handing it to Mahland, so he could throw them from the tailgate as we flew by each newsstand. He had quit school so he could go to work, as his mother needed the money. I was just finishing high school, but Mahland was nineteen and was drafted into the Army very quickly because he drew a very low number. He was sent to Fort Divans in Massachusetts for basic training and became an Army cook. We were able to see each other whenever he managed to sneak out on weekends until he was shipped out to Hawaii. On December 7, 1941, Japan bombed Pearl Harbor, and I never heard from him again. My last contact with him was a card he sent me from Hickman Field dated December 1, saying that he might be able to come home for Christmas. But my best friend was dead, and it was a very sad Christmas.

MY FIRST EXPERIENCE WITH MONEY as a great enabler came at the end of that year, when a little adventure led to a good deal of money, not only for a youngster like me but for anyone of any age at that time. It had started in October of that year, when a man by the name of Ed Miller, whom I knew casually, as he lived in our apartment building, asked if I could accompany him and share the driving on a trip to Florida in December. He owned a sign printing company in the neighborhood, and he was looking to get away from it all for a while and do a little gambling, as his wife had passed away a few months previously after a long illness. I agreed and, come mid-December, we were off to Florida. I preferred driving, and did I drive—the trip took a total of two days and one night.

On our first night in Florida, at the Red Hat Cocktail Lounge, Ed asked me to just stay out of the way and not annoy anyone, or sit at the bar listening to music and drinking the free beers. Ed paid for most of my expenses. I think he was lonely and this was his way of showing appreciation for my companionship.

On the second night I was bored, and the $18 of the $20 I had started the trip with was burning a hole in my pocket. I decided to take $3 and amuse myself playing the nickel slot machines. By the time the night was over I still had almost two dollars' worth of nickels in my pocket. The next night, I went back to the five-cent slot machines with my remaining nickels, and in about ten minutes I hit the jackpot and won $42.35 in nickels. This now gave me a bankroll of more than $50, which was enough to get me into the smallest poker game. I had been watching the big gamblers play the game and managed to come out ahead at the end of the night.

The next evening I decided to try my hand at the dice table. I had an incredible run and ended up walking away from the table with $417, quite a lot of money in those days. I was just itching to get into the biggest poker game. Ed, who was very happy to be even and ready to go home the next day, then watched me play in the big game, which ended with me playing an elderly man head to head. After several hours, the old man ran out of money and asked me if I would like to buy his car. It was an almost new, custom-built, 1940 Cord Convertible he had paid $2,800 for six months previously. He offered it to me at half that price. Without even looking at the car, I told him I would take it for $1,000, and he accepted. We continued the game and I was able to win back the thousand dollars that I had given him for car.

I now had almost $2,000 in cash in my pocket and a beautiful black convertible in the parking lot. At that point Ed and I decided to go our separate ways, both very happy with the outcome of our vacation together. He headed back to New York, while I went on to New Orleans for Mardi Gras. By the time I got there, however, I was too tired to participate in the crazy drinking, singing, and dancing in the street. So I just checked into a hotel, where a young $2 hooker who I gave a $3 tip relieved me of, among other things, the $300 in small bills from my back pocket while I slept. The next day I headed back to New York with my newfound wealth still largely intact. The $1,700 I had left would finance my educational costs and excessive personal spending for more than a year.

•••3•••

An Expert in Tubes

I WAS SUCH A POOR STUDENT that my parents never expected me to graduate from high school. They were anxiously waiting for me to get a job, as they needed me to contribute to the household. But I did graduate, and because I was such an outstanding ice hockey player, I was awarded a full-tuition scholarship to the school of engineering at Columbia University. The decision, go to school or get a job, was an easy one: I would go to college *and* get a job.

With World War II raging in Europe, the United States was substantially increasing its production of all sorts of military equipment. This created a nationwide shortage of workers; skilled workers, in particular, were in desperately short supply. The Sperry Gyroscope Company was advertising at my high school and interviewing students for immediate job openings as machinists. Just prior to my high school graduation, I interviewed with them and submitted an application. By this time we had changed the family name to "Howard" in an attempt to avoid the anti-Semitism that was rampant at the time, but without thinking, where the application asked for my religious affiliation, I wrote in "Jewish." The interviewer who took my application looked at it and told me there was no opening for me. I then went into another room with a different interviewer, filled out another application, and wrote in "Catholic." To no one's surprise, I was hired and instructed to report for work at the Sperry building at the foot of the Brooklyn Bridge in downtown Brooklyn two weeks later, just three days after graduation.

Although it was summer and I wouldn't start college until the fall, I requested the night shift, which ran from 11 p.m. to 7 a.m. Monday to Friday, so that I could also go to school when the time came. My parents were delighted with the job because I earned 40 cents per hour, for a total of $16 a week, half of which I gave to my mother.

The job came very easily to me, as I had been well prepared for it with the skills I learned first from Mr. Frank, my machine-shop teacher at P.S. 161, and later at Brooklyn Tech, where I excelled in machine-shop classes. One of my shop-class projects in high school involved repairing a small gas engine I found and adapting it for use in a model airplane, which I designed and built out of balsa wood and tissue paper. My 1937 delta-wing construction was ahead of its time. I received an award for this airplane but it did not have a remote control because such things did not exist at the time.

When fall came around and school started, I wondered if I had taken on more than I could handle, but it proved to be rather easy to both work and go to college. The problem occurred when the third part of my life, ice hockey practice, started after school. By the time I would go to work at 11 p.m., I was physically so tired that I had to be careful not to make mistakes milling the 30-inch diameter searchlights used for antiaircraft protection, which were my responsibility as a machinist at Sperry. I solved that problem by requesting a job change to that of a profile machine operator. This was a very simple machine to operate and required no precision measurements. You simply put a rough aluminum casting into a jig in the machine and lowered the cutting tool with a guide attached into the open portions of the jig so that the cutting tool underneath could remove the excess aluminum. This was a no-brain job that I could do when I was half-asleep, which I often was. Sometimes I would go into the men's room and fall asleep sitting on the toilet until the foreman kicked the door open and shouted, "Howard out!"

I worked the graveyard shift at the Sperry Gyroscope Company for two years during World War II, while taking classes in mechanical engineering at Columbia University. Those years went by quickly. But my personal finances were a real problem. The $8 that I kept from my salary was just not enough to pay for my books, gasoline, and other expenses at school. So whenever I was short of money, I would head out to Coney Island on Saturday nights and play for the Nathan's-sponsored, semi-pro ice hockey team known as the Hot Dogs. I earned $25 each time I played with them.

Later, I tried out for a position on the Brooklyn Crescents, a semi-pro Eastern League team. I played as a second-line defenscman on Sunday afternoons for two seasons. But I was involved in so many activities, including school, that my time and enjoyment playing hockey diminished substantially over those two years.

One of those activities involved my Uncle Jack, my mother's oldest brother, who had started a donut and malted-milk bar in downtown Brooklyn called the Sheffield Milk Bar. It was one of many innovative businesses that Uncle Jack conceived of over the years. For five cents, you could get a malted milkshake, and for an additional five cents, you could get two delicious frosted doughnuts. Chock Full O' Nuts would later adopt my uncle's five-cent milkshake and five-cent frosted doughnuts in their hundred or so shops in the New York area. So Uncle Jack retaliated by offering their five-cent cup of coffee and cream-cheese sandwich on date-nut bread. Since I passed by his shop when driving home from Columbia at night over the Brooklyn Bridge, I was able to earn $20 a week by removing the money from the cash registers and depositing it into a night box at the bank on the next block, while his employees cleaned up the store. A fringe benefit of this endeavor was that I could take home any or all of the delicious doughnuts remaining in the store at the time of closing. Having dozens and dozens of doughnuts to give away free to my friends the next day made me a really popular guy as well as quite a bit chubbier.

But eventually the pressures of school, life, and work got to me; something had to change and luckily it did. I happened to see a notice posted on the Sperry bulletin board, asking if any existing employees were interested in working at the new Sperry Research Facility, which had just opened in Garden City, Long Island. Since my parents had recently moved to Kew Gardens in Queens, which is close to Long Island, this new Sperry location made more sense for me than the one in downtown Brooklyn. I met with an interviewer, who said that one position they were looking to fill required an engineer with an intimate knowledge of tubes. As a mechanical engineering student, I thought she was talking about brass, steel, or aluminum tubing, so I said, "I know everything there is to know about tubes," and got the job because she knew even less than I did about them.

What the Sperry interviewer was referring to, however, was not metal tubes but vacuum tubes. The electronic vacuum tube lay at the heart of the development of electronics during the first half of the twentieth century. It was an extremely versatile device that could not only amplify audio signals but also generate, amplify, and detect high frequency signals such as radio waves. The vacuum tube had led to the development of radio broadcasting in the 1920s and 1930s, and would do the same for television in the 1940s.

Despite my lack of knowledge of electronics, I turned out to be just the person Sperry needed, as the people I ended up working for were actually looking for a person with machine-shop experience, which described my expertise perfectly. I was hired as an assistant to the Varian brothers, Russell and Sigurd, who with William Hanson had invented a vacuum tube called the klystron in 1937 that made radar possible. When the electrons in a klystron tube vibrate, it emits high-frequency microwave energy that can be detected by a radar receiver. The klystron tube would later be used in satellite communications, airplane and missile guidance systems, and telephone and television transmission.

Because of the war effort, Sperry had hired me as an engineer, even though I was only an engineering student. I transferred to Columbia University night school, and for the next ten years, attended as a paying, nonmatriculated student, taking only the electronic courses that I wanted and needed and avoiding nontechnical subjects.

Under the supervision of the Varian brothers, I set up a prototype manufacturing facility at the Garden City research laboratory. We manufactured approximately one hundred pre-production klystron tubes and presented them to be tested by the government agency in charge of this program. The test results were far better than their best expectations. As a result, the government agency allotted a large section of Sperry's new manufacturing facility, which had just been completed in Lake Success, Long Island, to producing klystron tubes. (This facility would become the first headquarters of the United Nations at the end of World War II.) Since I was the most knowledgeable engineer on the production of these tubes, I was assigned to the Lake Success manufacturing facility as the chief manufacturing engineer.

I managed to set up this facility in record time, but there were serious quality problems. Once production started, we had an unacceptably high percentage of defective tubes because one of the glass-to-metal seals had stress in the glass, causing it to crack after five to ten days of use, thereby losing the vacuum inside the tube. We went crazy trying to find the cause of that failure. But one teenage employee had no failures in her tubes so we had to find out why. The solution proved to be amazingly simple.

This nineteen-year-old, glass-blowing lathe operator was a tall girl with very long legs. I noticed that when she finished her operation, the blue torchlike flame did not go off immediately but momentarily turned into a soft yellow flame until she could remove her leg from under the lathe. Because her legs were so long and crammed under the lathe, once she finished the glass-to-metal seal, she could not completely release the gas pedal that heated the glass. This meant that the glass and Kovar metal seals in the tubes she produced cooled much more slowly and more uniformly together than those formed by other lathe operators and produced a stress-free glass with no failures. We learned that we could not depend on annealing the stress out of the glass in a separate operation afterward, so we adjusted all the lathes to the same slow-off flame. The mass production of the klystron tube then went so smoothly that I began thinking about how the klystron tube might be improved upon. But first a little personal matter would momentarily intrude on my career.

··4··

First Love and Other Minefields

MILDRED MARINO WAS MY FIRST LOVE. She was seventeen, gorgeous, tall like a model but much more zaftig (i.e. deliciously plump)—and trouble. She was a high school senior who loved ice-skating, ice hockey, and ice hockey players. I met her at the Brooklyn Ice Palace when I was skating leisurely at a public session one Friday night after practice. She quickly became enamored of me, my Cord car, my ice-skating, my ice hockey playing, and the fact that I had an important engineering defense job. We shared many of the same interests, including a very healthy appetite for sex.

I easily became a part of her close-knit Catholic family, which consisted of a grandmother who stayed at home and did the cooking; Mildred's mother, who was the breadwinner and worked six days a week; three older brothers who worked in construction jobs (two lived at home, one was married); and a sister who was about to get married. Mildred was the baby in the family and as a result everyone protected her. I had an open invitation to join them for dinner anytime, and I often did, enjoying a fine Italian meal with Mildred's family.

At one holiday party, we exchanged gifts. I bought her a high school graduation ring, which her mother had not been able to afford, and she gave me a St. Christopher medal with a matching silver chain for good luck. A few days later, when my mother saw the medal on my neck, she got so upset that she tore it off me. Dealing with Mildred afterward was just as difficult, but she finally accepted my explanation and gave me another one to wear, but only when I was at her house. Little did I know that my luck, which had never before required the support of a saint, was about to run out.

One weekday afternoon we were in Mildred's third-floor bedroom listening to records. No one was home except her grandmother, who was always in the basement kitchen cooking dinner, and she could not walk up the three flights of stairs. We decided to take advantage of the situation. But much to our surprise, her aunt, who was a nurse at the Kings County Hospital nearby and was not expected until dinner, arrived early, heard the music coming from Mildred's room, came up the stairs, opened the door, and caught us in the act. She started to scream. I don't know what she said, but I got my clothes on as fast as I could, ran out of the house, and drove away scared to death.

That night Mildred phoned to tell me that she had stopped her brothers from coming after me, but that they had insisted we get married in the Catholic Church the following weekend. That left me four days to decide what to do. I knew that getting married in the Catholic Church would destroy my Jewish mother. The only person I was close enough to to talk about my dilemma was Uncle Riley, who was a pharmacist and had a drugstore on Atlantic Avenue near the Brooklyn Ice Palace. I drove to his store as quickly as I could, and we sat and talked after he closed up for the night. We decided that the only thing he could do for me was talk to the brothers and try to reason with them. He called the brothers and arranged to meet them at a local diner at 6:30 the next morning.

The meeting was a disaster. Uncle Riley was shaken up and lucky to not end up in the hospital, as surely I would have had I gone to the meeting myself. Uncle Riley said that if I did not marry her, my life would be in danger. Not only was I scared of Mildred's brothers, but I did not wish to face the family consequences if I were to marry her in a Catholic Church. Although I had an important defense job and a draft exemption until the end of the war, Mildred's brothers left me no alternative.

After another sleepless night, I decided to give up my exemption and volunteer for the Army. That morning at 9 a.m., I appeared at my draft board office, signed the papers, and insisted that I be inducted the next day. I was told to report to the induction center on Lexington Avenue and 40th Street at 8 a.m. the next morning. I offered to sell my Cord convertible for $300 to a neighbor in my building who had long admired it. He was thrilled and drove me to the induction center in the morning, just a day before my marriage deadline.

I WAS IN THE ARMY NOW.

About fifty of us were processed for induction that morning. We were told to remove our clothes and stand in a straight line. Several doctors started at one end, and spoke to and examined each man as they worked their way down the line toward me. Needless to say, everyone was accepted and, after we put our clothes back on, we were marched onto a bus to Penn Station and then put on a train. We had no idea where we were going, but after nine hours on the train and a one-hour bus ride, we arrived at Fort Eustis, Virginia, where for the next three months we would be in basic training for the infantry.

Despite my two hundred pounds, I was in fairly good shape, thanks to my hockey playing and ice-skating. Because I looked big and strong, I was assigned to be part of a Portable Mortar

Needing an escape, I joined the Army in 1943.

Team, which consisted of three men: one carried the barrel of the mortar, which was the lightest of the three parts; another carried the case of twenty mortars, which was a little heavier;

and the third person carried the mortar base plate, which was a lot heavier. Of course, I was the base plate carrier. After four weeks of physical and equipment training, we were scheduled for a thirty-mile hike. It was a humid, 95-degree day and I had to carry my normal equipment pack as well as the mortar base plate. I didn't think I would make it, but I did, although at the end, while standing at attention waiting to be dismissed, I passed out cold.

I managed to survive basic training and we were all looking forward to a two-day weekend pass when it was over. There was a bus waiting outside the gate to take everyone into town that day and most everyone was already on the bus by the time I arrived at the gate. One of the guards said that some guys were asking for me. I then saw Mildred's brothers standing by the entrance to the bus. After three months, they had tracked me down and found me. To save my skin, I decided to forgo my weekend in town.

I was then transferred to Camp Patrick Henry in Newport News, Virginia, which also served as a stockade for Italian prisoners-of-war, and assigned to the ordnance department, where I learned how to repair guns. About a month later, I happened to tell my commanding officer about my engineering experience. I had gone into the Army so quickly that they never given me a skills evaluation and just enrolled me as an infantryman. I was then assigned to a Joint Forces Radar Test and Evaluation unit, just a short bus drive each day across the Chesapeake Bay in Norfolk, Virginia. This was much more up my alley.

On weekends, I would take the ferry to Norfolk and visit my two uncles. Uncle Riley, who was like a father to me, had sold his Brooklyn drugstore and joined his brother, my Uncle Jack, who was the half owner of two amusement parks, one in

Virginia Beach, the other five miles away in Norfolk. During the day I would wander the parks getting anything I wanted and going on the rides for free. I loved being treated like the boss's son by everyone, which included the right to pinch the rears of the showgirls of the Norfolk park's burlesque show.

Then one day I received the best news in all my life: Mildred Marino had gotten engaged to a soldier. The threat from her brothers was over. Now the only threat to my life was being in the Army, but a curious turn of events would change that as well. One night, I began sleepwalking, stepped out of the barracks, and somehow wandered into the ten-foot space between the two barbed-wire fences that surrounded the Italian POW camp. One of the guards in a tower at a corner of the stockade saw me but did not shoot because he noticed that I had on GI-issued olive-green underwear, rather than the white underwear worn by POWs. He sounded the alarm and soldiers came and led me away. I did not wake up until they stuck me under a cold shower. I was admitted into the camp hospital for observation, and after a week I was called into the commander's office and told that I had some kind of sleepwalking disorder. Investigators had even called my mother, who recalled that she had caught me sleepwalking three times, once while I was climbing out of a fourth-floor-apartment window. The doctors recommended that I be processed for an immediate medical discharge.

While waiting in the Army hospital for my discharge papers to be completed and approved, I made numerous friends. Although I was locked up with security guards posted at my door at night because of my sleepwalking, I had free access to the wards during the day. Since I was not wounded or sick like most of the others, I was able to do things for them that they couldn't do for themselves and which may or may not have been by the rules.

One friend was Milton J. Shapiro, who later changed his name to Milt J. Shapp, started Jerrold Electronics (more about that later), and became a two-term governor of Pennsylvania. Another was Murray Sedrich, who like me was from Queens, New York. He was a gunner on a B-29 when it was shot down over Germany. He had managed to parachute to safety with a dislocated shoulder but ended up in a POW camp for two months, until he and two others managed to escape and reach Switzerland, where they were then turned over to the American authorities and flown back to the United States. Murray ended up at Camp Patrick Henry weighing just ninety-one pounds. After about a month of treatment, he elected to be discharged and, like me, was waiting patiently for his papers.

When the day came, Murray and I took the train back to New York, along with his girlfriend who had come down from New York to ride back with Murray. During the train ride, they decided to get married; I would be his best man at the wedding. We remained lifelong friends, playing poker together on Monday nights and golf almost every Saturday, until Murray, after several mild heart attacks, died at the age of fifty-five.

I WENT BACK TO WORK AT SPERRY after my brief stint in the Army. Since the mass production of the klystron tubes now operated without a hitch, I directed my thoughts toward how to make a better and cheaper klystron. It was obvious that the size of the tube and all of its glass-to-metal seals were very costly. I thought the answer was to build the tube completely in a glass envelope. But to do this, the tube had to be much smaller, and you needed to be able to distort or tune the cavity so that you could change the frequency of the system during use. To solve this problem I thought of using a wire that would get longer or shorter depending on the amount of amperage that was passed through the wire. Getting it to work properly proved frustrating. So much so, in fact, that I antagonized my superiors to the point that they transferred me to another project—the emergency manufacturing of a recently developed mine detector, which the Army needed desperately. The Germans had placed tens of thousands land mines to slow the advance of the Allied troops, and field use of a device known as the Polish Mine Detector had been shown to save lives.

To get the production quantities the Army wanted quickly, the task of manufacturing this mine detector was assigned to Sperry and six other companies. Westinghouse was the Army's prime contractor, but the requirements were far beyond their capacity. I think I was given the responsibility of manufacturing the mine detector for Sperry because I had the reputation of knowing how to get a job done. I was given a full package of specifications, a bill of materials, the list of parts, the blueprints, and a methods manual, which explained how the devices were to be manufactured.

Organization would be the key to outperforming the other companies, so I began by sorting the items in the bill of materials into seven different categories. I then went to the purchasing department and asked for two people who specialized in each of these seven types of materials. My project had top priority, so they had to give me all the help I needed. I then gave each group a list of parts and said that we needed fifteen sets of parts to build ten prototypes right away and they had to be prepared to provide a supply of 1,000 pieces a week for production immediately thereafter. The number one person in the group would attempt to acquire the parts through normal channels, while the number two person would seek a source for the parts from any place that had them, without restrictions or procedures, at whatever the cost, in case the number one person was having difficulty getting the parts. To expedite the process, we were given a special priority number as a government procurement customer to use for these purchases.

I gave each of my seven teams the same mandate: they were to give me two progress reports a week and come to me with any problems. My deadline for completion and testing of the prototypes and the start of production was four weeks. There were to be no engineering changes; it was to be built "as is," except for component or enclosure changes or substitutions. Only a few sheet-metal parts needed hard tools made specifically to produce them. For the molded outer case I found a plastics manufacturer (Bakelite was the only plastic available then) that could make a case by gluing flat thin sheets together to serve as the case for the first 3,000 pieces. In about five weeks we had four prototypes approved by the Army and we started production in a quarter of the time of any other company. For this accomplishment, I received a Letter of Commendation from the Department of Defense.

After doing such a great job on the mine detector, I thought Sperry would be inclined to let me pursue my ideas for a new klystron tube, which would use less power than the original and could be produced at a fraction of the cost. But Sperry said thanks, but no thanks. Management declined to fund my approach since the current klystron tube, which was being produced in large volumes, was so profitable for them.

It was time to move on.

··.5.··

First Patent

IN 1944, WHILE GERMAN ARMED FORCES began using the V-1 flying bomb against the United Kingdom, I decided to apply for a job at the Sylvania Electric Company, which was located just two blocks from my parents' home in Kew Gardens, Queens. Sylvania was looking for experienced people as well as new innovative projects for their new R&D facility, so when I went for my job interview, I presented my low-cost klystron tube idea to the vice-president of engineering, who also happened to be the head of facility. He immediately took the bait and I was hired in 1944 as an engineering project manager in their advanced development laboratory.

My first project was the new klystron tube. Sylvania had the know-how to produce glass-enclosed vacuum tubes, so I designed my klystron to go inside a glass envelope. With the knowledgeable engineers of my Advanced Development Group, we brought the project to a successful conclusion in less than five months. Sylvania would end up producing huge quantities of this tube for the next thirty years. It did not become obsolete until 1981, when it was finally replaced, like all vacuum tube devices, with a semiconductor.

I liked working at Sylvania during the day and attending Columbia at night, but I intensely disliked the subway train ride between Kew Gardens and school. I had a car but I couldn't afford the cost of the gas each day, which at that time sold for about 35 cents a gallon. My sister's husband, Murray, who was the chief radiologist at the Kew Gardens General Hospital, came up with a solution. Murray told me that it would be a great service if someone could provide same-day delivery of a few envelopes of his X-rays and written reports to the local doctors. So each day after work I would pick up the X-rays from his office, which was only a mile away, and deliver them to the doctors in the neighborhood. This took me about thirty minutes each day, after which I could drive my car to school instead of using the subway, thanks to the $5 a week Murray paid me to make the deliveries for him.

One day, while waiting in Murray's office for him to finish a report, I saw that he was having difficulty reading and analyzing an X-ray because some white lines on the film were obscuring parts of the image. These lines were caused by an image-enhancing device called a Buckeye Grid, which would admit only the X-rays going in a vertical direction and absorb the radiation coming in at an angle. Though the Buckeye Grid offered much sharper X-rays than those of other systems, which were not as focused because the X-rays came onto the film at slightly different angles, the stationary Buckeye Grid left a series of lines on the film, shadows really, that covered about 20 percent of the x-ray image. Despite this drawback, the x-ray films produced by the Buckeye were still substantially clearer and better than those without it. The problem that no one had yet solved was how to get rid of the lines while still only permitting the vertical X-rays to come through.

I had the idea of moving the grid during the exposure of the X-rays so as to also expose the areas under the grid, thereby eliminating the shadows cast by the stationary grid and thus eliminating the white shadow lines. Murray and I tried this out by simply moving the grid by hand during an x-ray exposure, and it worked perfectly. There were no grid lines visible and the X-ray was as sharp as if the grid had been stationary. I then built a small sheet-metal frame for the grid to slide on, and used a small, heart-shaped cam, driven by a small-geared, one-RPM motor, which would be activated when the x-ray tube was turned on. The motorized cam pushed a spring-loaded film tray, moving the grid back and forth in a slow, continuous motion.

I filed a patent application for this idea, and one day, a salesman for Picker, which manufactured x-ray equipment, visited the radiology department at Kew Gardens General Hospital and saw what I had done to their machine in Murray's office. Shortly thereafter he told the story of my innovation to a friend who was an investor, and one day the investor and a patent attorney contacted me and offered me $1,000 for all rights to my patent application. I accepted it, as it was an enormous amount of money for me at that time in my life. This was when an engineering executive was paid only $350 a month.

DURING MY TWO YEARS as the manager of the Advanced Development Group at Sylvania, we had numerous innovative projects become rather successful products, mostly in the field of smaller, cheaper, lower power output products like the klystron. One very important military product that I supervised was an attempt to improve the reliability of shells shot from antiaircraft guns, which neither the British nor the Americans had been successful in doing. Antiaircraft guns fire thousands of shells, but only a miniscule percentage hit their target. Very often the shells would pass very near the planes they were intended to hit, but ended up either going off too far above or below their target because the fuze was preset in terms of time, distance, and altitude as it was loaded into the gun.

Then a new device came along, called the proximity fuze, which could sense when the shell was near enough to its target and explode. The shell contained a micro-transmitter that emitted at a specific frequency and used the shell tip as an antenna. Then, as the shell approached a reflecting object, an interference pattern would be created that would eventually trigger the detonation. The problem was that the klystron-like, ultra-high-frequency oscillator tube in the nose of each antiair-craft shell failed to operate more than 90 percent of the time when the prototypes were being tested. What was needed was a new tube that could withstand not only the high g-forces that were created by the firing of the shell but the centrifugal forces caused by the spinning of the shell as well.

Picked to be the project manager on this monumental task, I quickly recognized that we needed a way to subject the filament in the proximity fuze to g-forces while on a test bench in the laboratory. Out of this need I developed a vac-uum tube I named the Accelerometer that could ride along with the filament to be tested in a centrifuge. By simulating the forces of being fired in the shell on a test bench in the laboratory, we could quickly test many different designs and determine what needed to be changed to permit the filament in the fuze to work reliably when a shell was fired from an antiaircraft gun.

The problem was that, when exposed to g-forces and cen-trifugal force, the V-shaped filament in the proximity fuze would break because it was taut. The solution my team of engi-neers and I came up with was what I called the mousetrap fil-ament. Basically we attached a spring to the end of the filament, which gave the filament some flexibility. That way, when the shell with the proximity fuze was shot out of the gun, the mousetrap's spring would collapse and let the filament sag. But as soon as the shell stopped accelerating, the spring would snap back and hold the filament in its proper position.

The proximity fuze with my mousetrap filament was put to use in 1945, before the end of the war.

I WAS SOMETHING of a living proximity fuze myself, igniting whenever I approached an attractive woman. It was while working at Sylvania that I met my first wife. Lee was her name. I met her at a dude ranch where I would ride my horse, whose name was Timber. Lee worked in a lamp factory at the time but quit her job when our son Richard was born in 1947. Before long, I would put my wife to work in our little apartment, building some television sets for my first company.

··6··

Howard Television

PRODUCTION OF THE FIRST television sets had been suspended during the war. So televisions didn't become available in any quantity until 1946, when they were manufactured by two companies: RCA and DuMont. Everyone has heard of RCA but few people today remember DuMont, which also had its own TV station (Channel 6, WHNC-TV) and network shortly before the three majors, CBS, NBC, and ABC. There were very few programs available on New York City's three channels at that time. The programming consisted mostly of baseball games, wrestling matches, boxing, the 6 p.m. news, and occasionally, at 8 p.m., a variety show. Most of the day all you could see on TV was a test pattern.

Sylvania wanted to get into the television manufacturing business, but television CRT tubes were then in short supply. They were all round, measured either 7, 10, 12, or 20 inches in diameter, and used very thick lead glass, which produced huge distortions of the picture. And because the picture that was transmitted was rectangular in shape, the corners and the top and bottom of the picture would be cut off, or in getting the whole picture the image would be much smaller.

Upon looking into the problem for Sylvania, I found that one company, Corning Glass, manufactured all the glass envelopes for TV tubes, the sole exception being the 20-inch DuMont. Corning was trying to produce a rectangular-shaped glass envelope but estimated that it would be years before they could solve the problem of glass stress and implosion—if they could ever solve it at all. I thought we could solve the problem by making a cone-shaped metal envelope that would be rectangular on the large end, where the picture would appear, and round on the small end to accept the deflection coils and the electron gun. This approach would produce a nice, flat glass faceplate without losing the corners of the picture and without the distortion that occurred on the outer portion of the round picture tubes where the glass became substantially thicker. The other end of the picture tube I envisioned would look exactly the same as the round tubes already in production.

Sylvania agreed to build one hundred 16-inch prototypes of my rectangular picture tube to conduct the necessary production, engineering, marketing, and field tests. Though the results exceeded our expectations, the costs were too high and the yield too low. But our efforts did serve to stimulate Corning into more quickly developing a rectangular glass envelope at a modest cost. I would end up being the only customer for Sylvania's prototype CRT tubes.

Shortly after completing the TV tube project for Sylvania, I came down with hepatitis, a very serious illness. Even though I felt physically fine, the doctor ordered me to stay at home for three to four weeks. That allowed me just enough time to design and build a television set at home for myself. My plan was to buy and use one of Sylvania's prototype rectangular tubes and steal the circuit designs from the RCA patents.

One day I snuck out of the house and went to Canal Street in lower Manhattan, where all kinds of WWII surplus electronic equipment was being sold at a fraction of its original cost.

These surplus parts made it easy, fast, and cheap to get all the components I needed to build my first television set. As for the cabinet, that would come from Lou Horowitz, a cabinet manufacturer and close friend. Lou made an exquisite cabinet, similar to one that he made for a very expensive TV set sold by DuMont. I paid him $100 in cash for it, and into it I fitted the 30-inch tube chassis that I had designed along with the 16-inch rectangular Sylvania tube.

The first Howard TV set was produced in my one-bedroom apartment in Forest Hills with the front entrance foyer serving as my factory. I pushed the dining room table against the wall where I had hung a big circuit diagram, and on a tablecloth I placed all my tools and components and began wiring the chassis. Once it was assembled, I borrowed some testing equipment from the owner of a local radio repair shop who was interested in turning his shop over to the growing TV market. With his equipment and his help, I was able to do the necessary frequency alignment of the various circuits of my TV set, which contained thirty vacuum tubes. I must say that the final product was magnificent and the performance was second to none.

Whenever I was home watching television at night, some of my neighbors and friends would casually drop in to watch TV on my set. Only one friend in the same building had his own television at the time, an RCA with a 7-inch screen that he paid about $295 for in 1947. Then one day a neighbor offered me a thousand dollars for my TV set. Since it cost me about $240 in materials, I accepted his offer and delivered the set to him the following weekend. Immediately I bought the materials to build three additional sets and taught my wife, Lee, to do the wiring and fabrication by producing for her a color-coded, step-by-step sample harness on one of the sets and having her do the other two while I was at work at Sylvania. That was not a good

My two sons, Larry and Richard,
with a Howard Television set in 1959

idea. I ended up spending more time fixing her mistakes than
if I had done all the wiring myself.

Business was good and, as the demand for my TVs
increased, I decided to leave my job at Sylvania. But first I
needed to arrange to buy from Sylvania some of the prototype
rectangular picture tubes we had made. So I worked out a deal
with them. I gave Sylvania four weeks' notice, and agreed that
for three months after my departure, I would be available for
consultations with my group of engineers and patent attor-
neys to finish the project that we had been working on. As

compensation for these three months of consulting work, Sylvania agreed to give me, without charge, twelve of my prototype rectangular picture tubes. Afterward I would be permitted to buy more rectangular tubes from them at a fair price.

I handed in my resignation and ordered a dozen cabinets from Lou Horowitz and his Legion Cabinet Company for my first production run of television sets. When the twelve cabinets were delivered, we had to move the living room furniture against the wall to make room for the cabinets. But by the time I left Sylvania, I had rented a three-car garage as a factory space and hired people who knew how to assemble the sets. My wife was very happy to get all of the parts and cabinets out of the apartment. I was very happy as well: I had started my first company, Howard Television, Inc.

But almost immediately, disaster struck. While setting up my "factory," I went down to Canal Street and bought the materials and test equipment I needed for the twelve TV sets now scheduled to be my first production run. It was late when I returned from Canal Street, and I was tired, hungry—and stupid. I decided that I would leave my car on the street that night and not unload it until morning. The next morning I found my car window broken and all of the things I had bought on Canal Street were gone. I had just spent my last $2,400 on parts and equipment. I was in tears.

For the second time in my life, Uncle Riley came to my rescue. I just happened to have a lunch date with him; he was up from Virginia Beach visiting the family in New York. Over lunch I told him my sad story, and afterward he insisted I go with him to the bank. There, he retrieved his safe deposit box and took me into a small room. When he opened the box, I was amazed to see that it was filled with cash. Uncle Riley then said to me, take any amount of cash that you need, and when you can, you will put it back. His kind gesture saved my business. I took out exactly $2,400, which enabled me to purchase replacements for the parts that had been stolen the day before, and Howard Television was back in operation.

About six months later I paid him back the money I had borrowed and offered him a free television set to show my appreciation for his kindness. Little did I realize that my little gift would be one of the sparks that set off a whole new industry.

•••7•••

The Dawn of Cable Television

ONE DAY IN THE SPRING OF 1947, Uncle Riley walked into my Howard Television shop in Forest Hills and picked out his television set. Since he would not accept any interest for the money he had loaned me, I did not charge him for the set. He was planning on using it for his motel in Virginia Beach, so we loaded it into the back of his station wagon.

About a week later he called to tell me that he couldn't get reception, and offered me a free weekend at his motel on the oceanfront if I would drive down and troubleshoot the problem. So the next Friday afternoon I drove to Virginia Beach with my wife and Richard, our two-year-old son, for a free weekend on the beach. I discovered the reason he could not get any signal was because there were no television stations within 120 miles, the closest one being in Richmond, Virginia. I enjoyed my weekend on the beach and told my uncle that I would try to come up with the solution to his problem.

On my way back to New York on Monday morning, I stopped off in Philadelphia to discuss the situation with Milt Shapp, whom I had first met in the hospital at the end of my Army service. Since then I had heard a great deal about him and his company, Jerrold Electronics. He was using war-surplus vacuum tubes to build single-tube amplifiers for use in fringe areas where the television signals were weak. We discussed my uncle's problem in Virginia Beach and came up with the idea of cascading five of his single-tube boosters and then tuning the unit to the frequency of the one broadcast channel in Richmond. We thought we could solve Uncle Riley's lack of reception by using this amplifier to boost the signal strength thirtyfold and putting up a high-gain antenna atop a light pole in his parking lot.

Back in New York, I designed a high-gain antenna tuned to have the greatest response for the Richmond station. TV antennas at that time were made of thin, quarter-inch aluminum tubing. But I had heard of two brothers in the Bronx who manufactured aluminum chairs out of five-eighth-inch-diameter, thick-walled aluminum tubes, which I thought would be perfect for Uncle Riley's antenna. When I visited them, they agreed to make it for me, and in less than two hours they had the first single channel Yagi antenna made for TV ready to go. A Yagi antenna is a directional antenna, which takes its name from one of its Japanese inventors.

I arranged to pick up Milt Shapp in Philadelphia early the following Saturday on my way down to Virginia Beach. We arrived at Uncle Riley's motel with a five-tube amplifier, a 1,000-foot spool of coaxial cable, a 500-foot spool of zip cord (110-volt extension cord wire), the special television antenna that I had designed and had made for this purpose, as well as a compass to aim the antenna in the right direction. Both of us were afraid to climb the 30-foot light pole in my uncle's parking lot to install the antenna and connect the amplifier, but since I was fat and Milt was in good shape, it was Milt who climbed the pole and installed the antenna and amplifier equipment. After a nervous three hours, we plugged in the power and, lo and behold, we had a beautiful picture of a baseball game from the channel in Richmond. This was the only television set with clear reception in the Virginia Beach–Norfolk area, and from that day on, my uncle's motel lobby was jammed with people watching television, and his rooms were fully booked.

About a month later, my uncle called to say the mayor of Virginia Beach and a few of his neighbors wanted to buy my television sets and have them connected to his antenna at the motel. So the next weekend, Milt and I again drove down to Virginia Beach with three line amplifiers and three television sets. We charged each customer $1,500 per set, including the connection to the motel's antenna, using the additional amplifier as a booster. We ran our coaxial line along the street, from one street light pole or utility pole to another, securing the coaxial cable to each pole with standard electrical tape, which, though illegal, was done with the mayor's blessing. Our customers were very pleased with the result.

Of the $1,500 each person paid, Howard Television kept $1,100 for the set and Jerrold Electronics received $400 for amplifiers and cable. Both companies were very happy with that arrangement. Although our system was made obsolete a couple of years later when three stations came on the air in Norfolk, our innovative installation was the beginning of a new industry—cable television. Milt, who was a very creative engineer and businessman, immediately recognized the industry's potential and decided to focus on the design and manufacture of innovative cable equipment hardware. My focus, on the other hand, was on the operation of a cable television system. I could see that once you had a franchise for a location and sufficient subscribers to cover the overhead nut and the front-end equipment and installation costs, you were faced with a sustained income, virtually forever.

The person who would help me turn that germ of an idea into reality was a walk-in customer named Ed Dennis. In 1948, he had spent a good deal of time visiting the Howard Television office in Forest Hills and talking to someone he thought was a salesman for the company. After asking many questions about our products and how the company had come about, he bought one of our most expensive sets, the one with the Sylvania 16-inch Rectangular Metal Picture Tube. Two weeks later he came back to tell the salesman how impressed he was with the performance of his TV set. He then told the salesman that he wanted to meet the owner of Howard TV. That salesman, of course, was me.

Ed had a proposition in mind and invited me to come by his office in Glen Cove, Long Island. His office turned out to be in the huge real estate office of Gross-Morton; Ed was their attorney. He then restated how impressed he was with the quality and incredible performance of the Howard TV set as well as with my knowledge of this emerging industry's problems as it gained momentum. He then explained that Gross-Morton was planning to build several large apartment complexes. The first one, which he showed me a model of, was called Windsor Park. Located in the Bayside section of Queens, New York, Windsor Park consisted of 18 six-story buildings with 120 apartments in each building. He wanted me, as a consultant, to come up with an innovative plan to satisfy the television antenna needs of the tenants. The firm was concerned that if each tenant were to install a television antenna on the roof, all those antennas would make for a monstrous appearance and perhaps damage the roof as well. Gross-Morton wanted to find a way to have one, or in any case, no more than a few, antennas on the roof of each building, which the tenants in the building could share and all get proper reception.

Fortunately, I now had some experience under my belt that would enable me to consider such a project. With the help of Milt Shapp of Jerrold Electronics, I had just completed the installation of the system in Virginia Beach, where we connected eleven customers to the antenna that Milt and I had installed for my uncle outside his motel. I asked Ed if I could borrow an unused office, excused myself, and got on the phone with Milt Shapp. Together, over the phone, we figured out that if we ran a single coaxial cable to each apartment, we could design and build the equipment that would amplify the signals from an antenna specially tuned to each of the seven TV channels available in New York City. We could then mix the signals together and use an electronic distribution device to split and isolate the signal for each individual apartment. At the time this was nothing more than a dream in our minds. Nothing like this existed; nor did anyone else have the expertise to design and manufacture such a complex system, which would later become known as a MATV, or Master Antenna Television system. The MATV is essentially a mini-cable system relaying the broadcast channels to all the apartments in a building or small housing estate.

It would take a great deal of trust and confidence on the part of Gross-Morton to take the risk and use a couple of ballsy young engineers for such an important project. The selling job became even more difficult when I informed Ed Dennis that we would need about $500,000 to $600,000 for the 18-building Windsor Park project, or $230 to $275 per apartment. We estimated that we would need a cash advance of half the total cost, or about $300,000 upon signing the agreement, in order to develop, test, tool, and produce all the equipment necessary for all the buildings, in accordance with Gross-Morton's schedule of construction. In 1948 this was a significant amount of money; it would not be handed over to us easily. So I called Milt Shapp and told him to get in his car immediately and drive up from Philadelphia so we could meet at Howard Television and prepare a technical feasibility analysis, and an economic justification, so that we could sell our ability to undertake this huge technological challenge. We were scheduled to make our presentation before the entire Gross-Morton organization two days later.

All I can say is that two days later Milt and I walked out of the Glen Cove offices of Gross-Morton with a signed contract and a $300,000 check. We did not know what a monumental task we had undertaken until Milt and I started to program the details of the project. We decided that Milt would focus on the design and manufacturing of the seven-channel amplifier and the distribution units (the electronic splitter/isolation units), but these were not needed for another year. I would focus on the installation of the coaxial cable to each apartment as they were being built and the subsequent installation of the equipment as Jerrold completed it.

But there was a little hitch to get around first. All the electrical work for the new buildings of the Windsor Park project had to be done by electrical contractors who were members of the electricians' union. As stipulated by the contract, these electricians would install the conduit to each apartment, which terminated in a small room on the roof where most of our equipment would be located. But since no one had ever installed a master antenna television system before, the electrical contractor agreed to let our men install the coaxial cable to each apartment, as well as the equipment to be mounted in this special room on the roof. They were happy to let us do this, as they did not want to bear the costs of complications that might occur by improper installation.

It took a number of meetings with various union officials, including the czar, Harry Van Arsdale, to pull this off, but we eventually arranged a most favorable contract for our company, the Electronic Installation Corporation. The union agreed to a new classification of manufactured electronic equipment, which for the first ten years, gave us the exclusive right to place a union-made sticker on all the equipment we manufactured and installed into new buildings, including the small television outlet plate in the living room of each apartment. At the same time, all of our employees would become manufacturing members of the union. In addition, I worked out a deal to avoid paying my employees the exorbitant rate that electricians were paid working on new construction jobs. On nights and weekends, when electricians were not on the job, my men would snake the wires to each apartment from the central point where the equipment would eventually be installed. Of course, to allow this to happen a substantial "thank you" was business-as-usual at the time. The attitudes, standards, controls, and laws toward such payments are quite different today.

Looking back on what we accomplished, I still find it unbelievable that we managed to complete a project of this magnitude, using technology that had to be created for this installation from scratch, in all eighteen buildings on time and trouble-free, providing clear TV reception on all seven New York channels to every apartment in every building. After we demonstrated the results of this system in the first few buildings of the Windsor Park project, Gross-Morton had us do another garden apartment development they had started called Windsor Oaks, which contained 320 apartments. For this antenna system installation we charged Gross-Morton less than half the price per apartment of the Windsor Park development, since the equipment had by then become much simpler and cheaper to produce.

While these installations were going on, Milt continued to do value engineering, which sought to reduce the cost of manufacturing while improving the quality of the equipment and the TV picture reception. I continued to negotiate exclusive new franchises, while training people to install and maintain the equipment that Jerrold was manufacturing. No properly trained manpower existed at that time. My training program enabled hundreds of young people to have a good job with a future. The cable television industry was just beginning.

As word spread of the success of our master antenna television systems business in New York City, I began responding to a huge number of inquiries from people interested in creating a franchise and installing the system in their community. For each project, however, we needed to negotiate an exclusive cable television franchise as well as get local participation in the financing of the project and political support for the system. We found that if certain key people in each community could profit in some way from the system, they would be most helpful to us. The next step was to negotiate to lease space on the existing poles that were owned by either the power company or the telephone company to enable us to run the coaxial cable throughout the community. There existed an old contract between the two that allowed them to use each other's poles for 25 cents a month rent. The maintenance of the poles was the responsibility of the pole's owner. We were able to force them to give us the same deal, 25 cents a month rent, as neither the power company nor the telephone company wished to renegotiate their old working arrangement.

At the same time we managed to make these installations a no-risk investment for us by coming up with a better financing plan that would offer pre-completion discounts on the connection charge. This policy of offering prospective customers a 20 percent discount for signing up before installation dramatically changed the way each franchise was financed. It substantially reduced our front-end cash requirements and, as a result, reduced the percentage of local ownership. Milt Shapp and I worked closely together to develop this business and create what would become a major industry.

The demand for cable television was so great that we were making more than three times the connections per mile than we had projected in our business plan. As a result, our cash flow from hook-ups and monthly maintenance charges was substantial, and the return on our investment was in months instead of years, which made it all that much easier to obtain outside financing for future projects. I was micro-managing every aspect of Howard TV and the cable system business at the time, but as the business became increasingly widespread and complex, I quickly became both physically and financially overstretched. I was in desperate need of skilled management help. I needed to create an organization that could take care of all the finances involved and hire partners who could take charge of each business.

Then, quite out of the blue, a friend of mine introduced me to two people who were perfectly suited for the task at hand. One was Irving Maturin, who had just sold his women's clothing manufacturing business. The other was Henry B. Lewison; a German refugee who fled to Britain in 1938, he had manufactured leather wristwatch bands in the United Kingdom and had recently immigrated to the United States. Both men were looking for new businesses with a future. Since they both had years of experience running their own companies, they were exactly what I needed: one, Henry, to be my "Mr. Inside," the other, Irving, my "Mr. Outside," who would watch the store and control the people as well as the finances.

So in 1949 we formed a partnership called the Electronics Installation Corporation. To keep them motivated, I gave each of them a small piece of every business with little or no investment on their part. That worked well for everyone. We continued this partnership for the next fifteen years. They made more money than they ever did in their lives, and since I didn't have to concern myself with the details of running a business, I was free to work or play at whatever I wanted.

Almost. One problem remained mine: the payoff to the local officials, which became standard practice and too quickly became a monumental problem for me, as I had to accumulate it personally. But I understood that I would have to continue this practice on my own, rather than expose myself to a number of legal and personal problems if I were to have my partners participate in the payoffs. So I handled the payoffs, which represented after-tax money out of my own pocket, without the knowledge or participation of anyone else. This was a wise decision, as I could have ended up in jail as one person who followed me in this business eventually did.

The cable system business had created an easy and lucrative opportunity for us, but by 1949 Milt and I decided to go our separate ways. He wanted to be in the equipment manufacturing business, and I wanted to be in the master antenna and cable TV system business. These were entirely different views as to where the best opportunities lay in this new industry.

···8···

A Barrel of Transistors
for Dr. Wang

THEN THE TRANSISTOR CAME ALONG and changed everything. Transistors would eventually replace the vacuum tube because they never failed, were very small, and used less than one percent of the power that vacuum tubes used.

The invention of the transistor in November of 1947 was something of an accident. Walter Brattain at Bell Labs had built a silicon contraption to help him study how electrons acted on the surface of a semiconductor, a solid material whose electrical conductivity at room temperature is between that of a conductor and that of an insulator. But his experiment kept getting ruined because condensation kept forming on the silicon. So Brattain dumped his whole experiment into a thermos of water. That got rid of the condensation. But it also produced the largest amplification he had ever seen. He and a fellow scientist named Robert Gibney stared as the result in disbelief. By fiddling with it, they discovered that a positive voltage would increase the effect even more. When their colleague John Bardeen was told what had happened, he got an idea for a new way to make an amplifier. When he applied electrical contacts to the silicon, he found that the output power was larger than the input. This new amplifier produced only a tiny bit of amplification—but it worked.

William Shockley, also of Bell Labs, saw the potential in this new amplifier and, under a research and development grant from the U.S. Navy, worked to greatly expand our knowledge of semiconductors. Today many regard him as the "father" of the transistor. But Bell Labs was not allowed to disclose this project to anyone other than the U.S. military. Several American vendors were taught the secrets of producing transistors to military specifications, and since the transistors were part of a secret government program, their manufacturers were not permitted to sell them to anyone other than the U.S. military. But as a new technology, the percentage yield of manufactured transistors that met military specifications was very low.

I came into the picture in 1950 when, during a United Jewish Appeal fund-raising function, I met at my table a fellow contributor who in the course of conversation mentioned that he manufactured transistors for the U.S. military. I asked him for his card and said that I would like to visit him at his plant in New Jersey. So the next morning I showed up at his plant without prior notice or an appointment, and with his card in my hand, I asked at the front desk to see him.

It was coffee-break time, so he met me in the cafeteria, since visitors needed a security clearance to enter the plant. We sat and had a cup of coffee and I told him of my need to convert my cable equipment to transistors. Unfortunately, he said, he could not sell them to me and it would be at least three years before he could. Then after a long silence, he said, "But..." He then explained that the rejected transistors that did not meet military specifications were thrown into barrels and sold as scrap for $150 a barrel. He said that he would sell me this scrap for $300 a barrel and suggested that I buy one barrel to see if I could use enough of these rejected transistors to justify the price. I quickly opened my wallet, handed him $300 in cash, and said that I could take the barrel in my car right away.

With a barrel of transistors in the back of my station wagon, I drove directly from New Jersey to Harvard University, where Dr. An Wang was a professor of physics. I had originally met him several years earlier, when a friend of mine who was attending Harvard graduate school told me that he was going to attend a lecture by Dr. Wang called "The New Phenomenon of Transistors." My friend asked if I wanted to join him because he thought that I would be interested, and I did. In addition to teaching, Wang ran a small R&D lab where he conducted personal experiments. When I reached Hartford, Connecticut, the halfway point of my trip, I phoned Dr. Wang and told him what I had in my car. He immediately made an appointment to meet me in his lab at 5:30 that afternoon; he was anxious to test some of the transistors.

Dr. Wang and I worked until two o'clock the next morning because the results from our tests of the transistors in the barrel were unbelievable. The quality of these transistors was better than our greatest expectations, and the yield from the barrel was running near 80 percent. This was a dream come true and Dr. Wang and I kept testing more and more transistors because we thought the yield would suddenly take a nosedive. It didn't.

The next day we decided to make a breadboard amplifier to test the transistors with actual television signals. Dr. Wang assigned that task to two of his graduate students who worked for him part-time in his laboratory. Three days later we had a working, single-channel amplifier that had a better signal-to-noise ratio than a similar vacuum tube amplifier.

I then took all of this information and equipment, together with half of the transistors, to Philadelphia and turned the entire project over to Milt Shapp so that he could start manu-facturing a full line of cable television equipment using these transistors, of which I now had an unlimited personal supply. Of course I made it clear to Milt at a meeting with our attor-neys that these transistors would be used exclusively in equip-ment that he would sell to me and to me only.

Dr. Wang had insisted on keeping the other half barrel of transistors so that he could start integrating these transistors into a product he was working on in his laboratory, a very com-plex scientific calculator. His plan was to develop these calcu-lators and test their market potential. This would permit him to get some financing and in 1955 start his own company, which he would call Wang Laboratories.

This was the beginning of my long business relationship with Dr. Wang.

··9··

Cashing In on Cool

IT'S TRUE WHAT THEY SAY about necessity being the mother of invention, but few people talk about the generations of off-spring that follow. Take the case of the Navy's large cannon turret cleaner, for example. During World War II the Navy had a problem with the huge cannons that fired 16-inch shells on their battleships and other large naval vessels: they couldn't figure out how to clear the air inside the large turret enclosures of all the smoke, dust, and debris that was released when these guns were fired. In the past, for the smaller cannons, the Navy had used a central system that filtered the air in the turrets, but as the guns became larger and more powerful, the air-cleaning problem became increasingly acute.

Then along came Alex Lewyt, who solved the problem with a new, canister type of air cleaner that was small and compact, about 14 inches in diameter and 10 inches high, and could filter a large volume of air in a very short period of time. The Navy could place one to as many as ten of these small, self-contained devices in each turret, as needed. The devices would turn on automatically once a gun was fired, very quickly clearing the air of all the debris in the turret. Navy personnel working to load and unload these guns needed only to hold their breath for thirty seconds or less after a gun was fired to avoid inhaling any gasses or debris from the turret.

After World War II, Alex Lewyt made some slight modifications to his canister air-cleaning device and turned it into a commercially viable home vacuum cleaner called the canister vacuum cleaner. The old, upright, cloth-bagged vacuum cleaner was no match for the convenience and suction power of the Lewyt Vacuum Cleaner. Because he was already in production with this device and could deliver large quantities quickly, Lewyt essentially captured the U.S. vacuum cleaner market in a heartbeat. But Lewyt was a one-product company at the time, so in an attempt to ensure the company's future, he diversified his manufacturing facility and decided to go into the room air-conditioner business, which like numerous other appliances was in enormous demand after the end of World War II.

Like his vacuum cleaner, the Lewyt Air Conditioner was unique and ahead of its time. I first read about through-the-wall installations of room air conditioners in a 1955 article in *Popular Science,* a magazine I had subscribed to since I was a kid. In its size and shape, the Lewyt unit was ideal for installation *under* the window of new apartment construction, which was booming at the time due to a newly passed federal mortgage financing law and the fact that no new apartments had been built during the war. For private homeowners, this solution eliminated the need to hang those big, unsightly air conditioners *in* the window.

Since we were already selling antenna systems to all the builders of apartment houses in the New York area, I thought we could use our connections to sell room air conditioners to them as well. It would give the occupants of these apartments individual thermostat controls in each room and be far cheaper for the builder to install as the buildings were being constructed than to do so afterward, even if the builder did no more than place a shell in the wall for the tenant to install the air conditioner at some future date. I knew that few builders would refuse, as air conditioning or optional air conditioning was a big incentive to renting buildings quickly.

I thought this was a good way to give Howard TV, which had made a decent profit on its limited sales for about decade, a much-needed shot in the arm. By the mid-1950s the company had begun to struggle because dozens of major U.S. radio manufacturers had become TV manufacturers. These big companies would become successful because they had the financial resources to work out all the technical, supply, and intellectual property problems involved in TV-set manufacturing. Their having the advantage of mass production facilities in place, as well as national and international distribution, made it virtually impossible for small manufacturers like Howard TV to survive in this increasingly competitive environment. I needed to work out a way for Howard TV to begin installing Lewyt Air Conditioners.

The first thing I had to do was establish a relationship with Irving Bottner, the CFO of the Lewyt Corp., so that we could become the exclusive distributor of these air conditioners in the New York metropolitan area where we had a very strong presence. I made an appointment with Bottner, who was also a member of the board of directors of the Lewyt Corp., and met with him the next morning in his luxurious office in the Lewyt building located in Long Island City. We talked for several hours and got to know each other rather well. We then left for a nearby Italian restaurant, and after a pleasant lunch and friendly conversation, we got back in my car to drive back to his office. But on the way to his office, he asked me to pull into a vacant parking space on the street, which I did. He then said, "Now let's you and I talk *tachlis*," which is a Yiddish expression meaning, "let's talk turkey." From then on, I called him "Irv."

We did talk turkey. He said that he would give us an exclusive distributorship for Lewyt air conditioners, but I secretly needed to give him the equivalent of a 10 percent ownership in this distributorship, which we would call Polar Distributors, Inc. I agreed and this relationship continued very smoothly for a couple of years. We sold over 100,000 Lewyt air conditioners during that period, but then many of the traditional window air-conditioner manufacturers, who were losing market share as a result of the widespread success of our through-the-wall air conditioners, came out with their own version of the Lewyt but at a more attractive price. During that same period General Electric came out with a canister vacuum cleaner similar to the one that Lewyt manufactured but at half the price.

With a slowdown in the market for both of their major products, Alex Lewyt instructed Irv to find a buyer for the air-conditioning manufacturing portion of their business. Since Irv was a 10 percent partner in Polar Distributors, he informed me of any offers or negotiations on their air-conditioner business. In thinking and planning ahead, I had contacted a local manufacturer who was in the business of making small, under-the-counter refrigerators as well as a complete kitchen unit that contained a refrigerator, stove, and sink. When I met with him and we toured his manufacturing facility and the Lewyt air conditioner facility together, he was very enthusiastic about becoming a custom job shop manufacturer of the Lewyt through-the-wall air conditioners for me exclusively. At the same time I quietly offered the chief engineer at the Lewyt facility a position with King Refrigerator Company, if and when I managed to buy the air-conditioner division of Lewyt Corp.

Eventually I was able to make a rather complicated deal with Lewyt that included assuming the entire contractual obligation for purchasing components as well as all of the material that Lewyt had in various stages of manufacturing. I had a tremendous advantage over anyone else making an offer for the company because, with the help of Irv, my partner in Polar Distributors, I was able to determine the exact worth of this package. The deal was made for about $.25 on the dollar of the true value of the equipment and components purchased. This gave me a very competitive cost-of-materials advantage in the marketplace, so I was able to sell the through-the-wall units for a lower price than Lewyt ever could and still maintain a decent profit margin. Lower overhead, lower cost of manufacturing, lower cost of product, and one less step in the distribution food chain enabled us to sell a product at rather competitive prices once again. This resulted in the sale of another 60,000 air conditioners over a two-year period, when once again the same dilemma of competition began to raise its head.

SHORTLY AFTER OUR ACQUISITION of Lewyt's air-conditioner division, Irv Bottner resigned from Lewyt and became the CFO of Revlon, the cosmetics company. Irv, who also became a member of the Revlon board, quickly became a personal friend of Charles Revson, the pioneering cosmetics industry executive who had created Revlon Cosmetics and managed it through five decades. About two months into his new position, Irv called me and said that we needed to talk about his share of Polar Distributors, as well as discuss some compensation for his role in our acquisition of Lewyt Air Conditioner.

When I visited him the next day at the Revlon Building, we sat and argued for several hours before reaching a compromise. I agreed to give him $30,000 in cash, although he was looking for a great deal more—$100,000—to settle all of my obligations with him. He agreed to give me at least a month to accumulate that sum in cash; $30,000 was a huge amount of money in 1959.

Once I had the money in hand, I called Irv to tell him I had what he was waiting for. He said he would take a taxi from the Revlon Building to my 10,000-square-foot warehouse building in Flushing, Queens, where my first-floor office had a view overlooking the street. About two hours later a taxi pulled up to the front of my building, and I saw Irv get out and walk into my office. He had a great big smile on his face when I greeted him. I then took him into my private office where I had a large safe in which I had already prepared the $30,000, all in $100 bills. I locked the door, closed the venetian blinds of my office, removed the brown paper bag containing the money from the safe, and asked him if he wanted to count it. His answer was short and sweet: "It looks like $30,000 and that's good enough of a count for me." Since the $30,000 in the paper bag could not fit into his briefcase, he took the paper bag in one hand, his briefcase in the other, shouted goodbye as he walked out the door, and vanished into the waiting taxi.

But when he returned to his office building on Sixth Avenue in Manhattan, he took his briefcase but absentmindedly left the brown paper bag with the money in it on the seat of the taxi. Apparently he was the last fare of the day for the driver, who then drove his cab to the terminal where the next driver began cleaning the back of the cab and discovered the brown paper bag. He took it and handed it to the driver just as he was walking away. When they looked into the bag and saw the cash, they shouted and attracted everyone's attention. The end result was that the manager called the police and turned over the paper bag with the money in it. Since the taxi driver had been waiting outside my office for Irv to return, the driver directed the police to my office in Queens. When the police simply asked me the name and phone number of the man who had visited me in a taxi that day, saying they just needed to ask him a few questions about the driver, I felt that I had an obligation to answer the police. I saw no harm in giving them Irv's name and phone number.

That afternoon I received a very angry phone call from Irv, who shouted at me for having given the police his name and phone number. He then told me why he was upset; he had unintentionally left the paper bag with the money on the floor of the cab when he returned to his office. Rather than try to explain to the police about the transaction that had taken place between us which resulted in this enormous amount of cash in a brown paper bag, Irv had denied that the bag belonged to him! He told them that he only had his briefcase when he first got into the cab and only had the same briefcase when he returned to his office. Giving up the money, he explained, saved us both a good deal of embarrassment and a lot of trouble. But when he suggested I should reimburse him for at least half of the $30,000 as a fair way to settle this matter, I, of course, refused. That, unfortunately, was the end of our friendship, at least until he retired from Revlon and came back to me later, looking to join the board of directors of one of my other companies.

BACK IN 1958, ABOUT A YEAR before competition began to threaten our air-conditioning business, I had an idea to combine into a single unit the through-the-wall air conditioner and a central hot water or steam heating system. This approach had the advantage of a low-cost, through-the-wall air conditioner as well as the low cost of installation and maintenance of a central heating system. So I began working with local radiator manufacturers to find an easy and inexpensive way of combining the two. The solution turned out to be rather simple. All we had to do was to emulate the existing fan coil units that were being used in central heating systems in apartment houses. What we did was place a fan coil unit in front of a through-the-wall air conditioner. Since no one had done this before, we started a separate company to manufacture the product and named it Cool Heat Corp.

I needed someone to manage this business and turned to an engineer by the name of Dr. Fred Jacobs, who was the chief engineer of the air-conditioning division of Welbilt Corp., a manufacturer of low-cost and low-quality window air conditioners. When we discussed the concept, he expressed sufficient interest in the product that we had him sign a nondisclosure form so we could show him the prototype we had built in our shop. He quickly saw the advantages of combining central heating with through-the-wall room air conditioners and was enthusiastic about taking on the position of CEO of this new company if he could have equity in the company. I agreed to give him a one-third interest in the company if he put up $1,000. For two-thirds of the company, I would provide the necessary financing and marketing expertise.

With the terms of the deal agreed to, we rented a building in Farmingdale, Long Island, set it up for manufacturing, and began production in about two months. Because we were already doing business with most of the builders and architects in New York, for either through-the-wall air-conditioners or master antenna TV systems, both of which were going into

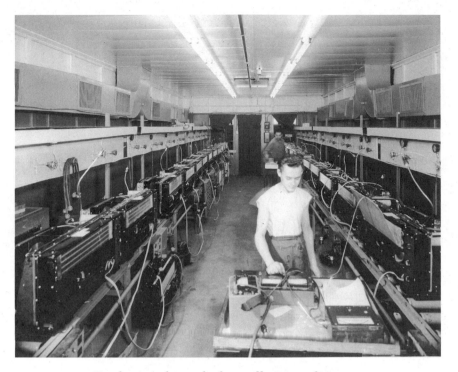

Producing through-the-wall air conditioners
at the Cool Heat factory in 1962

most new buildings, we quickly developed a substantial backlog of orders. We also received many inquiries about our product from builders throughout the Northeast. Profits rolled in
very quickly, and during our second year, after our financials
for the prior year were completed, Jacobs came to me to com-
plain. He was doing all the work running this business, he said,
and I was getting two-thirds of the profits. He thought this
arrangement was unfair and wanted to change it. I was sorry he
felt that way and offered him one of two solutions. Either he
could buy me out or we could sell the company.

When it became known that we might be interested in selling the company, an investment banker approached us to negotiate the sale of Cool Heat Corp. to Weil-McLain, a major

"comfort heating" company. We happily furnished our very up-to-date financials that went back to the first day we started the business. In a matter of just a few weeks we sold the company for a very favorable price and Fred Jacobs received one-third of the net amount of the sale. Additionally, he received a five-year employment contract to continue as CEO of the company as a division of Weil-McLain. But the demand for this product grew so quickly that the management of Weil-McLain decided to move the business to their main manufacturing facility in Utica, New York. Jacobs decided not move his family upstate, as he had just finished building a second home in very fashionable East Hampton, Long Island, and his wife and his three young children loved to spend their vacations on the beach in the Hamptons. So Jacobs stayed on Long Island and started a small mail-order business that never achieved worthwhile profits.

Years later I would receive a call from Fred, saying he was sorry that he was no longer associated with me. He then admitted how wrong he had been in thinking that our original arrangement at Cool Heat was unfair. After we sold the company, he said, he came to realize that I could accomplish more with just one phone call than he could by working hard all day. That was a very mature statement on his part, and three months later I offered him a position as an executive of a new company I was starting. This company, called Centronics Data Computer Corporation, would be one of my largest and most successful companies.

Though I had sold Cool Heat, I still owned Polar Distributors. When my son Richard finished college, he wanted to take over Polar Distributors, which I had promised to him years before for his dedication to working most of his summer vacations at Polar since he was about fourteen years old. There was one little hitch, however. Polar was principally in the wholesale room air-conditioner business and sold in bulk to builders; Richard had a bachelor's degree in arts and science. Since he had no technical education or knowledge of the business, I told him that he had to take a course in air-conditioning theory, service, and repair at a trade school, the Acme Technical School. He did so, and six months later he started full-time at Polar.

The business came quickly to Richard and I rarely had to intervene other than to deal with builders who now and then were not paying for their air conditioners in a timely manner. Over the years Richard changed Polar's business focus dramatically, from being principally in the room air-conditioner business, to selling to builders not only air conditioners, but gas ranges, refrigerators, and smoke- and fire detection equipment as well. It is now over thirty-five years later, and he is still running Polar and doing so more successfully than ever.

$\cdot\cdot\,10\,\cdot\cdot$

A Bust and a Boom

ANYONE CAN HAVE A BAD DAY. Not all my business deals turned to gold. One that decidedly did not was the Jalson Corporation. In 1958, my friend Lee Shey introduced me to his cousins the Kushners—Jay and his younger brother Sal. The brothers had an investment deal that required some additional money to buy an option for a square mile of land in Melbourne, Florida. The area needed low-cost housing due to the commercial boom caused by the construction of the new NASA facility at the Air Force's old missile range at Cape Canaveral (later renamed Cape Kennedy). The Kushners had received FHA approval to build one-family homes with three bedrooms and two baths that would sell for $8,990. The plan for this project, called Crown Heights, was to build 1,400 houses, as well as donate the land for a school to the town of Melbourne. This seemed to me to be a fantastic business opportunity for any investor.

Everything about the project looked as golden as Florida sunshine. With one exception. The only thing that I did not check on was the brothers' ability to build these houses to FHA specifications and make a profit. We had glossed over that little detail because of their experience building middle-income, custom homes on Long Island. But Florida was not Long Island. I decided to invest only in the land, which I would release a little at the time for them to build a few houses on. This would minimize my financial exposure, and I felt that owning land in this area was good sound investment. I was right about that.

The Kushners built three different model homes and furnished them. On opening day, after some modest advertising in local papers, they were mobbed. That weekend they took $5 deposits on more than 600 houses for the first section of this subdivision. That's all they asked for, a $5 deposit from each customer. Keep in mind that all that was required at the closing was $25 for the down payment, and the FHA would furnish a mortgage for $8,875, provided the purchaser qualified.

Soon after construction started, however, the Kushner brothers ran out of money and came to me to help finance their construction business. It was easy to see, when we checked their books, the reason they had run out of money: their cost for each home was higher than the selling price, and the partial-as-completed payments from the FHA were not sufficient to pay the contractors. In our subsequent discussions they convinced me that they had to build the houses as parts of a production line, with the contractors going from house to house without continually having to go back and forth, as they were doing now. Building one home at a time would never see a profit, they argued. The production line approach should substantially reduce their construction costs, without affecting the quality, because the FHA had to inspect and approve several phases of construction to see to it that the homes met FHA specifications. That's all the FHA cared about: construction specifications.

Convinced by their rationale, I foolishly agreed to finance the construction of the homes in return for a 51 percent ownership of their company, Jalson Construction Corp. What I overlooked was the fact that they only had experience building one house at a time; they had never done construction on a serial basis the way Levittown was built on Long Island. I quickly realized, after the first fifty houses or so, that the two brothers did not have, nor would ever have, the ability to construct 1,400 houses at a profit. As a result, I found myself having to go to Florida for a day or two every week to try to get some control over their operations. I finally decided that someone with the experience and skills necessary to complete this project had to be put in charge.

The Kushner brothers were violently opposed to this idea, but they eventually agreed to let me hire a construction manager who would have my authority in making any decisions that affected the cost of the project. The Kushners would restrict their activities to the preparation of the individual house lots with roads, water, and sewer provisions, and they could only continue in that role if their costs were on-budget and the delivery of these lots to the new construction manager remained on schedule.

Though it was a struggle, we eventually built the 1,400 houses. We only needed to wait for final FHA approval of the project in order to receive their payment on the balance of the money due to us. This money would be sufficient to pay all of the contractors and other construction obligations as well as pay me back the money that I had invested in both the construction and the land. We were a happy bunch the day the FHA inspectors were due to inspect the subdivision. So much so that we had planned a celebration.

We waited anxiously as the inspectors completed their task. We had even expected there might be a modest checklist of things to do for final approval of the project. But to our amazement, the inspector told us that since we had started this project, the specifications for this project had changed and that now sidewalks were required for the entire subdivision. They said that we had been notified about the change more than six months previously but apparently my wonderful partners either did not receive it, or more probably just did not read this notification from the FHA. All our plans to finish this job and pay off our obligations went down the tubes. What could do we do now?

There was only one solution. We had to find someone in the construction business who could use the tax loss involved in this project and who had the financial and construction ability to finish the job. When I returned to New York, I went to see several investment bankers I knew and asked for their help in finding a company that would fit the bill and take over Jalson Corp. In a few days, Billy Walters, who was the owner of Whale Securities, a small brokerage house that specialized in startup IPOs, had found a company in Washington, D.C., that appeared to be a perfect match to finish this project. We met with the two principals of the company and flew down to Melbourne with them the next day. They wanted to see the job firsthand and investigate the commercial potential of the surrounding land.

As they were analyzing their prospects for the project, I had time to gather some information on their company. Although they had had some very profitable years, they had faced some financial difficulties over the last six months. As a result, the stock price of their public company fell to about 10 percent of its previous value. I knew that they didn't have the cash to purchase this project; they could only offer their stock for this transaction. But I was prepared to accept any offer that would relieve me of the responsibility of paying for sidewalks for those 1,400 houses.

I wanted to get off the hook and out of Florida as soon as possible. So we made the deal for a large number of shares of their unregistered stock, which could not be sold for two years and then only in limited quantities every three months, under SEC rule 144.

With tongue in cheek, I happily accepted the deal and hoped for the best. But as I had suspected, the shares ultimately proved worthless. I decided that the entire loss in this transaction would be my personal loss. The only advantage I received was a tax savings to the extent of the loss because I was in a high tax bracket. This Florida experience, more than any other single event, made me a much more cautious businessman for the rest if my life. It was a lesson I would not soon forget.

As quickly as I could, I contacted everyone who had invested in this venture and had expected to make a substantial profit from it and told them what had happened. I informed them that I intended to pay back the full amount of their original investment as quickly as possible, and within one year I did just that.

THE STORY OF JUST HOW I was able to do so begins with a friend of mine by the name of Milton Gelfand. He was in the business of manufacturing master discs to make phonograph records. Actually, master discs are used to make the two pressing plates, which are the negative of the master and which when pressed together with hot plastic in between make phonograph records. Although it would take half a century before phonograph records would be replaced by compact discs, audiophiles still prefer the older style of recordings for their generally warmer sound quality.

Gelfand had a large facility, which created the pressing plates by electroplating copper onto the master discs. His innovation was to use nickel instead of copper to make the pressing plates. Since nickel is harder than copper, his pressing plates were able to produce more than twice the number of records that copper pressing plates could before they wore out. In addition, the sound quality of records produced from a nickel plate was superior, and that was a significant advantage because the record industry was moving into high-fidelity sound systems.

Gelfand was a chemist but he needed my help in designing the mechanical structure to hold and rotate the master disc while it was being plated with nickel. In order to plate a master disc with nickel, a device called the stumper had to rotate at about ten revolutions per minute with a little more than half of the plate submerged in the electroplating solution. I designed the mechanical structure in two days and Gelfand had six of them built in a local machine shop. Very quickly he had six plating tanks producing dozens of master discs made out of nickel instead of copper.

To test our new master disc, we went to a record-producing plant in Clifford, New Jersey. It just happened that at that time Chubby Checker was a very popular artist and his 1960 hit record started a dancing fad known as The Twist. Those records could not be produced fast enough. The master disc we produced with our new stumper was his latest hit song. I watched as the operator put pieces of black plastic on what is called a steam table. The operator would then turn the pieces of plastic over and over until they were hot enough to put on the press where the record was made. Preparing the plastic pieces on the steam table required more time than the actual pressing of the record itself.

We discovered that our new nickel master disc could produce 22 percent more records than the copper master discs. On the downside, however, with respect to the amount of time needed to complete the cooling cycle and remove the finished record, this process required three percent more time for each record. But the advantages of a longer lasting and better quality product substantially outweighed the disadvantage of a little longer cooling time, and the owner of the record company decided to start using nickel plates instead of the copper ones that were then in use.

Though we were successful with the new plates, I recognized that we had an opportunity to improve how the plastic material was heated and delivered to press. In the plastic industry, the method most often used for preparing plastic materials for further processing was to use an extruder. When I discussed this with Gelfand and the owner of the record factory, they both said that they had tried using an extruder a number of times and on all occasions it had failed. Why? The problem was a matter of temperature.

To produce an acceptable record, the temperature of the plastic at the moment of pressing must be between 200 and 220 degrees Fahrenheit; any cooler and the material is not viscous enough to pick up the information in the groves of the pressing plate, any warmer and the plastic begins to break down and smoke and produce an unacceptable record. The temperature of steam when it's not under pressure is 212 degrees; that is why the steam table worked so well to heat the plastic that was being made into records.

The problem was that the extruders in use at the time could not produce a plastic at a consistent temperature. In an extruder, the heaters located around the perimeter of the barrel from which the plastic emerges control the heat so that the plastic is heated to 210 degrees. But the friction that occurs in the extruder between the screw in the barrel, which forces the plastic through the barrel, and the barrel itself causes the plastic to gradually get hotter and hotter until the plastic breaks down and starts to smoke—at which point the plastic can no longer be used to produce a record. No one had been able to make an extruder that would produce plastic of consistent temperature in the range that would produce a quality phonographic record.

I thought the solution would be to have water flow through the center of the screw to prevent this overheating. So I came up with the idea of making the screw in the center of the extruder hollow, so that as the temperature of the extruded plastic rose to 210 degrees, water flowing into the center of the screw would remove the excess heat that was created by the friction of the plastic in the barrel.

To design and build a prototype extruder that would test this idea, I went to an extruder manufacturer located in Boston's technology belt, because at the time I was spending a good deal of time in that area on other business. The three engineers who did the design work told me that their company could not and would not take on a development project like this. But they offered to set up their own company to take on this project if I would pay them $10,000 in advance for the first extruder that they would manufacture to my specifications. They called the new company Gloucester Engineering, after its location in Gloucester, Massachusetts. I worked with them on a daily basis for about two months until the first machine was ready to be tested.

Gelfand and I and several of our associates were present for the first demonstration. On that eventful day, the machine was turned on, plastic pellets were put into the hopper, and the temperature was set to 210 degrees. After about ten minutes a beautiful, continuous, one-inch diameter strand of plastic started to come out of the one-inch diameter hole from which it would fall onto the dish-like surface below. The temperature, consistency, and appearance of the plastic that emerged was just perfect. But after just a few minutes the temperature of the material slowly started to rise. So I said, "Now's the time to turn on the water."

I went to the back of the machine where a water valve was connected to the rotating screw, and without thinking about controlling the amount of water, I just turned on the valve. Within about ten seconds, the machine exploded. Fortunately, since everyone was standing at the front of the machine and the explosion had occurred toward the rear, no one was injured. What had happened is that the water had cooled the plastic much too rapidly. This caused the plastic to harden within the barrel while our very powerful drive system kept trying to turn the screw. An explosion was inevitable. We all left the factory upset and very disappointed.

I couldn't get to sleep that night, as my mind kept searching for a solution. I kept thinking about the steam table, which worked so well because it could not get hotter than 212 degrees. Then the solution hit me: why not send steam through the center of the screw instead of water? Unpressurized steam has the ability to remove heat when the temperature of the surrounding area is higher than 212 degrees and to add heat when the temperature of the surrounding area is lower than 212 degrees. I thought I had hit on the perfect solution. When I told Gelfand and the three engineers of my idea the next morning, they were all eager to fix the extruder and have a new test. About ten days later, they had produced a new screw and barrel, and installed a new motor, all in record time.

This time the test was an overwhelming success. Now we had to give the extruder a reality test, putting it to use in a record plant with Gelfand's new nickel plates. Three days later we were ready to go. After the initial test, the owner of the record plant noticed that readying the plastic now took just five seconds but the operator then had to wait for the press to finish the record and remove it before using the next glob of plastic. The solution to that problem was an easy one: just let the operator run more than one press at a time. After numerous tests, the owner decided that the operator could run three presses along with one extruder. This produced a superior record at one-third the direct labor cost of the old steam table method of preparing the plastic. The $6,000 extruder, which cost us $3,000 to make, could pay for itself in production cost savings in less than one year. The economics were so good that the Clifton plant ordered twenty-six of the new extruders, and Audio Matrix Inc., which Gelfand and I owned equally, was in business.

The factory workers called the new extruder the Boomer, after a very famous man named Lord Boomer. There was an underground record at the time about a "passing wind" contest in England. The contest was presented as though the announcer was describing a prizefight, with the contestants farting on command. When Lord Boomer, the current World Champion Farter, came up to the Farting Post, the excitement from the crowd was enormous. If he could fart for four seconds, he would again be world champion. The announcer enthusiastically described Lord Boomer's fart, but when he was almost at the four-second mark, he shit. Since the glob of plastic from the extruder looked exactly like a pile of feces, the operators who used our extrusion machine called it the Boomer.

The Boomer was an instant success because the superior quality of the records produced with this equipment came at a time when the record industry was changing from 78 RPM to

33 1/3 RPM long-playing high fidelity records. As a result, we were overwhelmed with orders from almost every manufacturer of phonograph records in the country. At that point, RCA, the largest record manufacturer in this country, decided it would be cheaper to buy the company instead of ordering the huge number of machines they required. Just nine months after my original idea was tested and exploded, Gelfand and I each received $2.2 million after paying the capital gains tax.

And this is the money I used to pay back all those who had invested with me in the Melbourne, Florida, housing project. It all happened, you might say, in record time.

··11··

Family, Friends, and Photo Finishes

FOR ABOUT A DECADE, Lee and I and the children were a happy young family. After renting apartments from 1946 to 1953, it was exciting to move into our first house, a three-bedroom, 1,400-square-foot home without a garage in Bayside, Queens, that cost $19,500. My friend Lou Horowitz bought the house next door; he was making TV cabinets and I was his biggest customer. Life was busy and full. Lee was happy; she had a full-time, sleep-in housekeeper and a full-time, sleep-in nurse for the new baby, our second child, named Larry. She filled her time with a group of women neighbors who played cards three days a week, and another group of women who played Mah-jongg the other days of the week.

My parents came regularly to our house in Bayside to babysit Richard, during which time my father developed a wonderful and very close relationship with him. Together they would play a game called "The Judge." Since my father worked at the U.S. Post Office, he had a badge with the words "United States Government" embossed across the top. My father carried this badge in a black leather pouch and told Richard that he was a judge and that this was his judge's badge. In the game,

Richard was the bailiff and he would bring the criminals before my father and tell the judge what crime the person was accused of. Sometimes the criminals Richard brought before the judge were his little neighborhood friends who participated in this game.

Then, several years later, when he and his friends started to read, one of Richard's friends told him that his grandfather was not a judge, but a post office employee. Richard was broken-hearted because he thought that his grandfather was a real judge. The next time Richard saw my father, he went up to him crying and shouting, "You're a liar. You are not a judge. You're a liar." Richard then went to his room and cried for hours. My father retrieved Richard, worked things out with him, and was able finally to reestablish a warm relationship with him. Richard would later name his first son Seth, after my father, following Jewish tradition.

A NEIGHBOR OF OURS IN BAYSIDE at the time was Charlie Kalish. His wife played games with Lee daily, and I would spend hours looking at and enjoying Charlie's world-class antique pocket watch collection. Every watch he had in his collection had an interesting story, either about the person who made the watch or the person the watch was made for. The watches' complicated movements were of particular interest to me because I knew about the tools and machines that were available in the seventeenth, eighteenth, and nineteenth centuries, and it was difficult for me as an engineer to understand how such accurate and complicated mechanical devices could be designed and hand-built with the technology that existed at the time. This fascination with the tremendous accomplishments of these old watchmakers drove me to become a very serious antique watch collector myself.

It all started when I helped Charlie sell his photo-processing business. He owned the only lab on the East Coast that could reprint color film from one millimeter size to any other, from 8mm to 16mm, or to Super 8mm from any other. He had designed and built the machine that could do this himself. Coincidentally, I knew Ben Berkley, who owned the country's second largest photo-finishing network of labs after Kodak at the time, and I thought that Berkley might be interested in Charlie's company. It would be a way to make Charlie's local service available nationally.

My relationship with Ben Berkley had begun over something called the Color Film Negative Analyzer (CFNA). I was at a party for his much younger brother in the mid-1950s, when I met and had a long conversation with Ben. I learned a lot about his business because he liked talking to someone who could comprehend the technology involved. The 35mm color photograph market was exploding at the time, and he was having a difficult time expanding as fast as the opportunity presented itself. He explained to me that each individual snapshot he printed had to be color balanced to compensate for the color characteristics of each batch of film and the paper on which the picture was printed. This operation, which had to be done manually in a photographic darkroom, was the bottleneck that prevented him from growing the output of the entire factory. He also showed me the literature on a very expensive Color Film Negative Analyzer that would solve his problem, but he needed 50 of them and wondered if they could be made any cheaper.

I proposed using an entirely different approach from the existing CFNA that would end up reducing the cost of a color photograph as well as improving its quality. I suggested doing it all electronically. I could design and build a color film analyzer using the capabilities of the just-developed digital computer and some low-cost, black-and-white video cameras with a rotating color separating disc, divided into thirds for each of the three primary colors. The computer had to be programmed to color-correct each of the variables and do so quickly enough to register each color and analyze it during the short time that one-third of the disc passed by the lens of the camera. I found a group of consulting engineers in New Jersey who were hungry for work, and they were happy to take my conceptual design and build a prototype from it. The price they quoted me was very reasonable, so the price I quoted Berkley was double that amount, which he thought was reasonable. He then gave me half that amount as a deposit for the prototype.

The Color Film Negative Analyzer I developed for Berkley Photo in 1960

The engineers in New Jersey did a great job. There were some delays, mostly due to software and timing issues. As a result, we had a working prototype in eight months instead of the six months they had promised. Now we were ready to test this prototype at Berkley's main lab on East 19th Street in Manhattan. It took two days to set up the analyzer and get acceptable results on the finished color prints. Unbelievably, 99 percent of the color prints were acceptable using this machine versus the 91 percent rate when a person made the adjustments manually. In addition, the output of the automatic CFNA was almost double that of manual adjustment. This gave Berkley an enormous cost and competitive advantage over Kodak. I was compensated with a 50 percent bonus and an equal amount for all the rights, drawings, intellectual property, and know-how for this product, a bonanza I shared equally with the engineers in New Jersey, which made them very happy. Ben Berkley also asked me to join the board of directors of Berkley, a position that taught me a great deal about how public companies are run.

Now back to my neighbor Charlie Kalish. I did help him sell his business to Berkley, which proved to be a good deal for all parties involved. After the sale was completed, Charlie wanted to show his appreciation for my help by buying me a new Cadillac, but I refused to accept anything for helping him, which I had done as a friend. Charlie then came up with a great idea. He gave me two beautiful books on watch collecting, as well as an exotic pornographic watch I had admired for years. He also promised to take me, every weekend for a year, to see the watch collections of other collectors, as well as introduce me to the community of serious collectors all over the world. That's how I became a collector myself. Now, some fifty-five years later, I own one of the finest antique watch and clock collections in the world. This has been an exciting hobby, which has brought me great pleasure all of my adult life.

OUR DAUGHTER, ELLEN, WAS BORN in 1958 and about a year later, we bought a beautiful, two-story, 4,200-square-foot colonial in Country Estates, an upper-middle-class group of homes being built in Roslyn, Long Island. The house, which cost $35,000, had five bedrooms upstairs and a large backyard. That meant the children each had their own bedroom. The fifth bedroom was set up as a small gym with a couple of pieces of equipment. In the basement we had a full-size pool table that, once a wooden top was placed on it, could also be used as a Ping-Pong table. As was the custom in those days, we also built a bedroom with a bath in the basement for our sleep-in, full-time maid, who was paid $35 a week. Country Estates was a wonderful environment and neighborhood for children since almost everyone had one to four children, and most of them were about the same age as our three children. That fall, Richard started as a freshman at Roslyn High School, one of the best high schools on the East Coast.

I was hoping that Lee would now become more interested in my life and do more than just drive the kids around and play cards. There were more affluent and successful people in this neighborhood than there had been in Bayside, Queens. But Lee quickly settled into the same routine; she found a new group of women who also just wanted to play cards all day. At the same time, I made friends with a group of men who had much in common with me and together we started to do things independently of our wives. I joined the Woodcrest Club, a new golf club about fifteen minutes from my house, and enjoyed playing golf with them every Saturday and Sunday morning.

The winter came and in late December we had our first snowstorm, which brought us more than two feet of beautiful flaky snow. The house was built on a hill, and I took advantage of this by putting the garage on the down side of the hill so that the playroom I had built over the garage was on the house's main level. But that meant that out the front door was a steep slope down toward the street. Larry, who was then seven years old, took advantage of all the snow that day and was making a snowman on the lawn near the street. From the window of my study I could see that he was unable to lift and place the large head on top of the snowman. I decided to run out the door and help him, not realizing how slippery the lawn was under the snow. As I stepped on it, my right leg flew forward and my 250 pounds came crashing down full force on my left leg, which folded under me, dislocating my knee and tearing the muscles attached to the kneecap.

One of my son Larry's snowmen, which brought a 250-pound man to his knees

It was Sunday, and the only doctor available to receive my call was my sister's husband, Murray Fuhrman. After telling him what happened, he sent an ambulance to take me to Kew Gardens General Hospital where he would meet me. When I arrived he was waiting with the chief orthopedic surgeon and the operating room was almost ready. But since it was Sunday, they were one doctor short, so Murray, although he was a radiologist, assisted in the operation to reset my knee and reattach the torn ligament on my kneecap. Since I had finished lunch just before the accident, during the operation I gagged on my own vomit, choked, and stopped breathing. Murray said that he had to put a breathing tube down my throat, a procedure he had only witnessed a few times during his medical school education. He was particularly nervous since I was his brother-in-law and he was not sure that he was putting the tube in correctly. Murray knew that if I did not get any air for two to three minutes, I could suffer brain damage or die.

I survived the operation and had to have a hard cast on my entire leg for six months. But for at least ten years after that, there were times when my left leg would not bend at the knee, and I had no alternative but to get into bed as soon as I came home from a hard day's work. I would have my dinner in bed and watch TV with Larry, which I did whenever I was home. About seven months later, after some remarks Larry had made to me and others about my accident, we concluded that he felt guilty about being the cause of my accident and subsequent suffering. As soon as I realized that, I made up a story and told it to him at the appropriate moment, when we were chatting alone in my bedroom. I said that he had actually saved my life. If not for this accident, I told him, I would have been on that Eastern Airlines flight to Florida that had crashed in the Everglades and everyone aboard was killed. So his snowman had saved my life. He broke out in tears instantly, as though the weight of the world was taken off of him. Larry has kept me company throughout my life, and to this day we have a very close, loving relationship, despite some trying times.

MY LOVING RELATIONSHIP WITH LEE did not last, however. Although we would not divorce for another decade, our marriage had virtually come to an end by 1961. We shared no interests and had nothing in common. Our interaction was limited to going to a movie, having dinner out, or doing something with the kids. She did not develop into the kind of mature woman that a successful businessman needs to have as a wife and companion. As a result, each year we grew further and further apart. I needed companionship and I did not get it at home. That's the story that most successful businessmen will tell to justify having a girlfriend and cheating on their wives, but that scenario was true and justified in my case. The only reason the marriage lasted as long as it did is that I felt an obligation to stay with her for the sake of the children. So by 1961, I had become a part-time father and a husband with extramarital relationships.

What I enjoyed most during this time in my life was playing golf. I found the atmosphere friendly and being away from business and family pressures a real treat. The Road Runners, as we called ourselves, played every weekend morning. The regulars consisted of Sam Weiss, Murray Sedrich, Max Hugel, and Irving Gershon; the irregulars were Bill Casey and Sol Dashue. Most of these people would end up playing a large role in my business life and personal life.

Sam Weiss was the founder of Rayco, an auto seat-cover retailer with more than a hundred shops in the tristate area. Sam lived in the house behind ours. He had a girlfriend that he set up in an apartment on West 58th Street in Manhattan. She had a girlfriend named Brenda, who shared the apartment with her. The end result was that Sam and I shared the cost of the apartment and the girls went with it.

Murray Sedrich became my closest friend after we met in the Army hospital in Virginia and had been discharged together. He was a half owner of Nemo Ceramic Tile Co., a business started by his father and his father's brother, whose son now owned the other half of the company.

Max Hugel was the founder and president of Brother International Corp., the exclusive worldwide distributor of all the products of the mother company, Brother Industries Ltd. of Nagoya, Japan. They were the largest manufacturer of sewing machines and typewriters in Japan at that time. He would be of enormous help to me some years later when I invented the dot matrix printer and started a company called Centronics.

Irving Gershon was a world-renowned architect and a senior partner in the architectural firm of Emery Roth, which was responsible for some of the most innovative and challenging projects in the eastern United States. Irving was the lead architect on the famous Pan Am Building, which was built over Grand Central Station so as not to interfere with the trains. We were such good friends that he made me the executor of his will. Irving was a single parent whose daughter had a serious drug problem. When Irving died of a heart attack in 1966, I did my best to care for his daughter with what remained of her father's estate, but before long she died of a drug overdose. I think that if Irving were alive today he would be very proud of his son, who is now a successful architect, married with two children and living on Long Island.

Whenever one of the Road Runners could not play, which

was actually quite often, we would ask Bill Casey to join us. Bill was a war hero, a famous lawyer, and soon to be the head of the Securities and Exchange Commission. He could not be a regular because he was not consistently available, and although he was not very good at the game, we always enjoyed his company. Bill would become Ronald Reagan's campaign manager in 1979 and a year later, the director of the CIA. Max Hugel, who wound up working as Bill's assistant in the Reagan campaign, was appointed deputy director of the CIA in 1980.

Finally there was Sol Dashue, who was also a member of the Woodcrest Club and a regular nonmember of the Road Runners. Sol's wife, who played cards with my wife, thought that her husband was a member of our golf game, but that was only a cover-up. Instead he would spend every Saturday and Sunday morning at a nearby motel with his secretary-girlfriend. This went on for a couple of years, until one day his wife found a motel key in the pocket of the pants that she was taking to the cleaners. To see whose name the room was registered in, she drove to the motel and discovered that the room was registered under my name, Mr. and Mrs. Robert Howard. When she confronted Sol with her discovery, he told her that the key was indeed mine and I was going to use the room later that day for a secret business meeting that I didn't want Lee to know anything about. He told her that he was sworn to secrecy, and now that she knew about it, it would be very embarrassing to him if Lee found out about this meeting. So he pleaded with her not to say anything to Lee. Fortunately, this passed unnoticed, just like a hundred other such incidents.

ONE OF MY NEIGHBORS IN ROSLYN at that time was Jerry Kiviet. He had three kids the same ages as mine and a wife who played in one of Lee's card groups. Jerry had a yarn manufacturing business in the Bronx that, he said, had gone broke because his partner had been stealing from him for a few years and covering it up with false inventory figures. Now his partner had disappeared and his family suspected he might have committed suicide. Jerry said that the factors and creditors had closed the factory and were preparing to auction everything, including 10,000 square feet of yarn-spinning machines. The factors were a kind of bank used mainly in the garment industry; they loaned money to businesses that was secured by accounts receivables, inventory, factory equipment, and anything else they could get. Jerry said that he could make a deal with the factor to avoid the auction and buy everything for $75,000 cash on the spot; although it was worth over $1,000,000, there were no buyers. He convinced me that he was the only one who knew how to use the equipment and run the business, and proposed that I offer the factor the $75,000 and then take the yarn-spinning machines and have them rebuilt while he sold off all the miscellaneous equipment and yarn. Once the spinning machines were rebuilt we would find a building and get back into production.

It sounded like a good yarn to me. The novelty yarn business was booming and supply was limited because knitted women's clothing was all the rage. For my investment of $75,000, plus an additional $175,000 to pay for rebuilding the machines and setting up the factory, we would be partners and share everything equally after Jerry's $25,000 salary. Instead of renting space, I decided that I would buy a new building that was available at a bargain price from the bank, which had foreclosed on it two years previously. I had the personal net worth to support the mortgage and I made the rent a triple net lease so that

"Brentwood Yarn Mills, Inc." paid for the building and I got the depreciation to save on taxes.

All went as planned. We set up the factory in Brentwood, Long Island, which had a large Puerto Rican population who were happy to earn the minimum wage of $1.25 an hour, since most of the farm jobs they had been doing during the war had vanished. This was good for us because workers in the Bronx were being paid twice as much and were not as hard-working or reliable. This model was ideal for a profitable business, and as a result the company showed great profits for about two years.

What I did not know was that it was Jerry, not his partner, who had done, and was still doing, the stealing. His partner had run off with another woman when he was confronted with a business and personal bankruptcy and an unhappy marriage, so it was easy for Jerry to blame him for stealing from the company. Jerry was receiving kickbacks from the same suppliers he had always used.

What made matters worse is that Jerry had started gambling on sports and going to Las Vegas on junkets as a high roller. This meant that he had to steal a lot more to cover his losses. Since one-half of what he stole was his, he would have to take twice as much as he needed. He also used the money to secretly take over a bankrupt company in Connecticut and set up his oldest son to run the business.

When I figured out what was going on, I served him with a Notice of Deposition that took over a year and gave him the time to move everything of value to the Connecticut factory, take all of our customers, and not pay any rent or taxes. Even when he was gone, I was left with a building full of obsolete spinning machines that I could not remove because I did not own them. This legal dilemma took another nine months to resolve before I could start to clean out all the junk he had left behind, plus another year until the building was sold.

This episode had a very serious effect on the way I did business in the future. It taught me that a leopard cannot change its spots, and that doing business with friends was not always a good idea.

··12··

Shedding Pounds and a Marriage

MY HIGH-PRESSURE BUSINESS and personal lifestyle meant that by 1964 I had been hospitalized twice for chronically bleeding ulcers. Now I needed an operation to remove a section of my stomach, but doctors refused to operate because I was much too heavy; they said I would not survive the operation unless I lost a great deal of weight. Since 1960, when I had dislocated my left knee, I had added 30 to my usual 250 pounds.

My brother-in-law, Murray Fuhrman, again came to the rescue. He was one of ten doctors who had been first to volunteer for a new diet created by Dr. Walter Kempner. Murray had been on Kempner's Rice Diet since 1945, when he was given only three months to live because he had untreatable high blood pressure. Murray advised me to stop work and go down to Duke University in Durham to begin the Rice Diet immediately. Despite its name, the Rice Diet is really a low-salt, low-fat diet that involves eating fresh fruits and vegetables, grains, fish, and beans. Murray called Dr. Kempner and made an appointment for me at the Duke clinic two days later.

I gathered together my business associates at work, and then my family at home, and told everyone that I had to lose seventy-five pounds before the doctors could operate on me. I said I would be gone for sixty to ninety days, spending the entire time at a clinic at Duke. I would speak to them each day on the phone, or more often, if necessary. That same day, I packed everything that I might need for a long stay. I had expected to be hospitalized, so my office and my partners were prepared for my absence. I kissed my wife and three kids goodbye.

At 6 a.m. the next morning I was in my car and on my way to Durham. Murray had booked a room for me at a small, dingy motel on the outskirts of town, explaining that there had not very much to choose from. The motel was about two and a half miles from the Rice House, the only place I would be permitted to eat or drink anything while I was on the Rice Diet. The two-and-a-half-mile hike to and from the motel to the Rice House would provide some much-needed exercise and would also serve to fill up the long hours between meals and the social gatherings at the Rice House each day.

I arrived at Dr. Kempner's office the next day promptly at 9 a.m. His office was in the basement of Duke University Hospital, one of the largest in the South. I spent about an hour talking with the doctor and his female assistant, Dr. Pishell, while they took my medical history and delved into both business and personal matters, including the details of my sex life. I was then given a schedule, together with two pages of special instructions for the physical examination, which would keep me totally occupied for the next three days.

The morning after the tests were completed, I had a meeting with the doctors who reviewed the results and told me that my health was much worse than I had ever realized. My excessive weight and stomach ulcer were just the beginning.

They added diabetes, high blood pressure, thyroid problems, elevated cholesterol, and very advanced arthritis to my list of problems and scared the hell out of me. They certainly convinced me of the urgent need for a change in my eating habits. I had no choice but to focus more on my health and physical condition than I ever had in the past.

Being alone in Durham, living in a motel, and having a ratio of about ten sexually starved young women to each man on the Rice Diet was almost like going to heaven without having to die. Most of them were young women who had become chubby or fat, and were sexually neglected because of their weight. Eventually, once they lost some of their excess weight, they started to look attractive and were eager to try out their new bodies. In a number of cases I was the happy beneficiary of their experiments. This activity replaced the boredom of being alone and having nothing else to do but watch television every night.

Although I had a car with me, I would walk the two and a half miles to the Rice House each morning. Before breakfast was served, a team of doctors arrived, took everyone's blood pressure, weight, and a urine sample for analysis. My breakfast consisted of half a grapefruit, a wedge of lettuce with only vinegar and pepper as dressing, and a multivitamin tablet. The Rice Diet limited me to just 800 calories a day.

At that time I was an extremely good golfer with a seven handicap, and the golf course at Duke University was one of the most magnificent in the country. Each day, immediately after breakfast, I would walk the two miles to the Duke golf course with three other good golfers who were also Rice Diet patients and play most of the day, either eighteen or thirty-six holes. For lunch I would have an apple, which I would eat while playing. This allowed me to save most of my 800 calorie a day allotment for dinner at the Rice House. After all, I needed my strength for my evening activities.

After golf each day, we would stop off at the YMCA, play some volleyball, and go for a swim. Then we would shower, shave, put on some fresh clothes, and head back to the Rice House. Dinner was a big social event, during which all the patients gathered together and compared notes about how they were faring on their diets. We tended to focus on our evening activities at this time, rather than the meal, which involved little more than a small portion of vegetables with no taste, and a dessert, either a small piece of fruit or diet Jell-O. I was careful not to let anyone know who would be coming to my room at the motel or whose room I would go to each night. Keeping this a secret was critical to being able to play the field.

This was my life for sixty wonderful days that passed much too quickly. I lost sixty pounds in sixty days at Duke. I looked and felt like a new person and hated to leave. With new pants and sports jacket at the going-away party that my girls held for me, I looked twenty years younger. After my first stay, I would go back to Durham about once a month for a few days for what I said was a check-up, but it was actually fun and games. All told, I was on the Rice Diet for two years and eventually lost one hundred pounds. Thanks to Dr. Murray Fuhrman, Dr. Walter Kempner, and the Rice Diet, I am healthier today than I was when I started the diet in 1964. Even today, more than forty years later, I follow the Rice Diet 75 percent of the time.

My stay in Durham was one of the most enjoyable in my life. I felt like a single man again. In this environment, I was able to forget, for a limited time, about home, family, business, and all my other obligations. I met and had encounters with many women there, but one was particularly important. I met Enid Badler during the last week of my first stay at Duke. She was

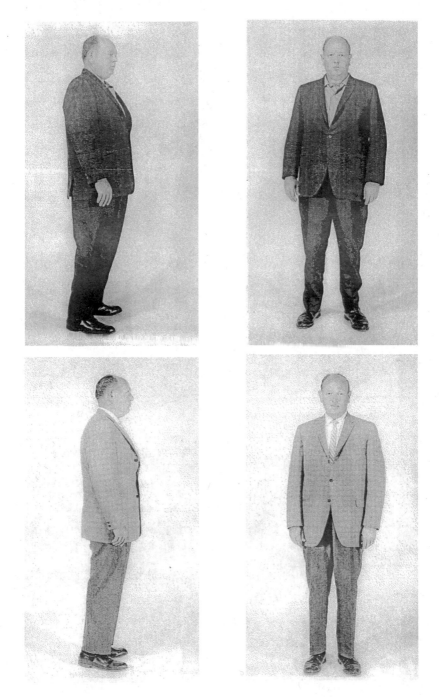

Sixty pounds in sixty days: Before and after shots showing what I lost on the Rice Diet at Duke University in 1964

an unhappily married woman who had been at Duke for six months. She eventually divorced and worked in real estate for a while. I don't know how much she weighed when she started the diet, but when I first met her she was 136 pounds and looked great. This was the beginning of a sexual friendship that continued each time I went to Duke, then moved on to Long Island where I would visit her while her children were in school, and later took place in New Hampshire where she came to work for me until 1973. She had what I would call the gift of gab, so the position that best suited her in my company was in the public stockholders relations department. She would take calls from obnoxious shareholders and try to pacify them. She was quite good at it. The problem was that by the time she started working for me I was about to be divorced from Lee and getting married to a woman named Lenore.

I met Lenore during a long weekend golf trip to Florida with another friend, Marty Cohen. We happened to run into two married women from New York who were alone on the golf course, and in the course of the game we cooled off together under a tree as we waited for a slow foursome in front of us. While waiting, Marty suggested that we become a foursome. During the game we all joked around and had a lot of fun playing the game. When we found out that their husbands would not arrive in Florida for another three days, we quickly invited them to join us for dinner that night, and they accepted. After dinner we went back to their hotel rooms in case their husbands called and we stayed late or all night with them. It was a great beginning to three wonderful days in Florida.

About a week later, back in New York, I received a call from Lenore. She wanted to meet at a restaurant and have lunch. She was a "shopping bag" decorator, meaning that she didn't have an office or showroom for her interior design business but carried her fabric samples in a shopping bag. If anyone saw us together, she could always say that I was a client. At that time I had business in Boston and she pretended to have business there too so she could join me for a day or two. This went on for about two years. One day we were speaking on the phone and she forgot to push the privacy button on her phone, which enabled her daughter, who had come home from school early, to listen in on our conversation. The sixteen-year-old later spoke to her older brother about this overheard conversation, and they in turn decided to inform their father. He then hired a private detective to follow her and report on her activities. It was very easy to substantiate the fact that she was having an affair with me. One evening he confronted her, told her to pack her things, and threw her out of the house.

I received a frantic, almost incoherent, phone call from her at about 1 a.m. when I was asleep next to my wife in the bedroom. It was very difficult to have a conversation with her. After the call, I told Lee that I had to go to the office because I thought we had been broken into. I got dressed and left. About an hour later I met Lenore in Manhattan and she proceeded to tell me what had happened. We found her a place to stay for the night and discussed looking for an apartment for her to live in. Later we would sit down and find a long-term solution to her situation. We both had spouses and children to consider in making this decision. It was about 5 a.m. when I returned home, and I went directly upstairs to the bedroom and took a shower. When my wife woke up, she asked me where I was going so early. I said I had to go up to Boston for a few days and would call her tomorrow. That was the beginning of the end of my marriage to Lee.

About a week later, I packed some things and told Lee that I had met someone else. She was surprised, saying that she thought we had a perfect marriage. We waited for Larry and Ellen to come home from school that day and sat down with them to explain the situation very carefully so that they understood that they had been the glue that had held us together for the last ten years. But as I look back now, I think that my decision to stay with Lee for twenty-four years was not a wise one.

I made it clear to the children that I would always be there for them, both emotionally and financially. I would always take care of them, as would their mother. Richard was about to finish college and take over the business of Polar Distributors. He was seeing a young lady from Brooklyn by the name of Lois, and they were planning to be married in about six months. Larry was attending The George Washington University in Washington, D.C. Ellen was still attending Roslyn High School and would be living at home with Lee.

In coming to a financial settlement with Lee, I agreed to give her the alimony she requested along with child support for each of the three children, even though only one was still living at home with her. For my peace of mind, I also agreed to continue these payments to her as long as she lived, whether she remarried or not; I did this because I felt that she would never remarry. I very quickly moved out of the house and into a furnished rental apartment in New York City. I had packed all of my personal and historical memorabilia into a carton and left it in the corner of the basement to be picked up once I had found a permanent residence. Unfortunately, about a year later, Lee thought the pile in the corner was garbage and threw it all out. That's why I no longer have photographs of my illustrious days as a hockey star.

In any case, my new life was now about to start.

$\bullet \cdot \cdot 13 \cdot \cdot \bullet$

Howard Hughes and the New York City Cable TV Franchise

MEANWHILE, MY CABLE TELEVISION BUSINESS was flourishing. The arrival of the transistor had signaled the start of a whole new era for the cable television industry. The use of transistors instead of vacuum tubes was an incredible competitive advantage for us—at least until transistors became available to everyone else two or three years later. That head start, however, was enough for us to literally capture, for a time, the entire cable television industry. The use of transistors instead of vacuum tubes in a cable system not only reduced the initial cost of installation by half but also significantly reduced the cost of maintenance by 90 to 95 percent. That was a very significant economic advantage since the monthly charges to stay connected to the system were based on the high cost of maintaining the vacuum tubes and included bringing to each piece of equipment the needed 110-volt power source, which was sizable compared to the minuscule power requirement of a transistor—just 5 volts— and that could be provided on the same coaxial cable line as the television signal.

Once the cable business began gaining acceptance outside major metropolitan areas, and the technical problems were solved to the point that subscribers were now willing to pay for something that was better than either poor quality reception or none at all, we could now think of going after big fish, like a New York City franchise. But like the telephone and the electric companies, we needed an exclusive to protect our investment in the infrastructure, which was considerably higher in New York City than elsewhere because all the wiring had to be done underground and the cost to use the existing underground conduits ran more than four times the cost to do aboveground wiring. On the other hand, the cost per subscriber was much lower due to the concentration of people in the city. So the end cost per subscriber was a fraction of our usual cost to deliver the TV signal using power and telephone poles to distribute our signals from building to building.

I was still looking for a way to eliminate the need for having our expensive front-end equipment, which consisted of an amplifier for each television channel and a distribution system, in each and every building where we installed our master antenna system in New York City. Using technology from my cable companies, I applied for and received an experimental microwave transmitter license so that I could transmit New York's seven local channels from the George Washington Bridge toward midtown Manhattan, where there were hundreds of very large apartment buildings in need of sharp, ghost- and interference-free TV signals. With just one front-end setup on the George Washington Bridge we could receive and retransmit a microwave signal containing all seven of New York's channels to a receiver in each building or an entire square block of buildings. There the microwave signal would be converted back to the normal seven-channel analog signal. This would enable tens of thousands of customers to get a clear picture at a fraction of the cost of a wired distribution system.

It was a great idea and worked well until CBS sued us for retransmitting their copyrighted material contained in their local Channel 2 transmission from the Empire State Building. That litigation put an end to our George Washington Bridge project, but it made me famous when I said during a court deposition that within twenty years over-the-air broadcasting would end and be replaced by cable television because of the large bandwidth it permitted compared to over-the-air transmission.

Since microwave rebroadcasting was no longer an option, the only other way to bring clear television reception to much of New York City at reasonable cost was to have a cable-system franchise. Since the city was corrupt, it was easy for me to get to the properly connected individual who could talk turkey about our plans. After a dozen meetings, we came to an agreement about who would get the required payoffs and when. Only once that was accomplished could we start to negotiate the terms of the franchise and those negotiations proved to be quite difficult. In the end, in order to consummate the NYC franchise, I had to give the city a $5 million franchise fee, as well as line the pockets of a number of politicians. To deliver this hefty fee, I had to bring in other risk-taking investors who shared my business vision, since I was at the limit of my personal financial resources. Selling a piece of the New York City franchise was the only way to help defray the initial cost of a business that had enormous potential. New York City was a juicy plum for a cable TV system operator because of the huge concentration of a generally wealthy people. But that kind of start-up money was not available from venture capitalists at that time, and for a while, it seemed as though I would never find the money needed to close the deal, especially since others were trying to break up the New York City franchise into at least five segments, one for each borough.

But again my lucky star shone bright, and along came a prospective investor out of the blue. A Wall Street friend who knew of this business opportunity introduced me to John Meier, who was on the lookout for investment opportunities for Howard Hughes. After two days of talking and answering a million questions, Meier suggested that I come to Los Angeles with him on one of Hughes's private planes to meet with Robert Maheu, who was the real decision maker for Howard Hughes's investments.

John Meier worked for, and reported only to, Mr. Maheu, who was a Mormon and one of the very few people directly in touch with Howard Hughes. Actually, by this time, Maheu no longer spoke to Hughes; they communicated only through handwritten messages scribbled on standard yellow legal pads. But that rather cumbersome means of communication didn't prevent us from making the deal in one day. Hughes agreed to pay seven million dollars for 50 percent of the stock of my New York City cable TV franchise company, and John Meier would be on our board of directors. This was another marriage made in heaven. After the lawyers worked out the details, we all signed the documents, and I walked out with a seven-million-dollar check.

Tom Dewey was the attorney who represented Hughes in the deal and I was rather disappointed to see how inept he was, especially as he was once governor of New York, though he did lose the presidency to Harry Truman in 1948 in the greatest election upset in American history. Dewey was quite old then, and after we signed the deal, I hardly heard a word from them. I did send them a monthly financial report and only occasionally received a phone call from Bob Maheu with a question. There were also two or three unannounced visits from John Meier, probably because he happened to be in New York on other business anyway, and he did attend our annual board meetings.

WITH A LOT OF HARD WORK, all went well with my New York City cable franchise and most of my other businesses until 1964 when I returned from the Duke Medical Center. I wasn't scheduled to return to the office immediately after my two months on the Rice Diet in Durham, North Carolina, but I did anyway. I went into the office on a Saturday afternoon without the prior knowledge of anyone in the company. In the process of just looking around, I saw on the desk of Henry Lewison, one of my two partners, an envelope attached to a sheet that contained a list of building addresses, apartment numbers, and dollar amounts. The total of all the dollar amounts represented the amount of cash in the envelope. It wasn't hard to figure out that this list of transactions was cash collected from subscribers for the additional coaxial cable that ran from our TV outlet in the apartment to their set. They were charging an extra 25 cents a foot beyond the six feet they were supposed to furnish at no charge. This was an unauthorized charge I knew nothing about; I had never participated in this cash income. Although I had no way of knowing how long this had been going on, there was no doubt in my mind that it represented a substantial amount of money.

I put everything back as I had found it, locked the doors, and went to a Radio Shack store to purchase an expensive, sound-activated telephone recording system. I then returned to the office and installed this wire-tapping, automatic recording, telephone listening device on the phone line used only by Henry Lewison, the "Mr. Inside" of my management team. Again I left the office exactly as I found it, but I could now record his private conversations and listen to them at a later time.

Still without contacting anyone from the company, I went to our local bank on Monday morning and requested entry to our company's safe deposit box, to which both my two partners and I had access. When I opened the half-empty box, I found $106,000 in small bills. I decided to take all of this money since it probably represented but a small portion of what they had taken over the years. I then went back to Durham, North Carolina, to make it seem as though I had never come home.

A week later I telephoned and told everyone that I was coming home for the weekend. My wife, Lee, and my two sons came to pick me up at Newark airport. Walking down the long corridor, I saw the three of them approaching, so I put down my carry-on bags to be able to hug the kids. As I stood up, the three of them walked right past me without recognizing me. That's how different I looked after sixty days on the Rice Diet.

That afternoon I went into the office and removed the tape that contained the recordings of Henry's private phone calls. In the evening I listened to the conversation between Henry and Irving about what to tell me about the $106,000. I had enough evidence to confront them and start legal action, but our business relationship was so complex that it would have been the wrong road to follow.

On Monday I went into the office where Henry Lewison and Irving Maturin confronted me about the $106,000 missing from the safe deposit box. They knew that I had taken the money from the safe deposit box, but they did not know about the wiretap of Henry's phone. They understood that I knew something but not exactly what. I asked them to explain the origin of the money in the safe deposit box. They gave me some Alice in Wonderland story and I let them think that I believed them. I knew that I could use the tape at any time to gain an advantage and get whatever I wanted since they broke the law, and I had the hard evidence. But I decided to consult with my attorney first, as I did not want to be thrown into the fire with them. Unfortunately, they knew that I had made a number of questionable business deals myself, so I decided that the best approach to resolving this problem and disassociating myself from these two individuals would be to sell all of the companies they managed and/or were partners in as quickly as possible.

Over the next four years, I quietly disposed of a total of about fifteen companies. Since I had a controlling interest in most of these companies, I could force this to happen. Some of the companies were active, some just produced income, and some no longer existed. They included Electronic Installation Corp., Windsor Park, Windsor Oaks, Gyro Electronics, Amplitell, Acme TV, LeFrak City, Jalson Construction, Municipal Sewer & Water Corp., Riverview Corp., Lewyt Corp.'s air conditioners, Cool Heat Corp., and various community cable system franchise corporations. During those "sale years," I watched Henry and Irving like a hawk and fired the head bookkeeper who had helped them hide the cash and who was having an affair with Henry Lewison on a fold-up cot in the office either before or after normal business hours.

We sold a large group of cable system companies, including the New York City franchise, in 1964, and the rest two years later, to Teleprompter, which at the time was a troubled company whose principal product was being replaced with a better, cheaper, computer-driven teleprompting device. Teleprompter was run by Irving Kahn, a flamboyant, 300-pound businessman who was a great negotiator, a fancy dresser, and a gourmet. He started by refinancing most of our old franchises and upgrading the equipment. He did so well that the Teleprompter stock I received from the sale of my companies grew from the $2.00 a share I received in 1964 to more than $42 a share when I sold it in 1967, about a year after the sale of my remaining cable system companies to Teleprompter.

But as a result of a normal SEC filing examination, the cash payouts Teleprompter had made for various cable television franchises was discovered. That triggered a full SEC investigation and eventually Irving Kahn, the president and CEO of Teleprompter, was found guilty and sent to jail for bribing Johnstown, Pennsylvania, and other city officials with $15,000 in the course of obtaining the franchise. Kahn had foolishly disregarded my advice and put on the books of his public company the cash payments that at the time were standard practice for obtaining a cable franchise.

But while in jail, he proved to be smarter than all of us and made some very intelligent acquisitions of several underfinanced cable franchises and MATV system companies in New Jersey. At the time, many small cable systems were being acquired by the few major cable companies because, as the technology continued to improve every six to twelve months, the companies needed strong financing to continually upgrade their cable equipment for better picture quality and cheaper, more reliable, and much lower power requirements. By the time Kahn got out of jail, after serving just twenty months of a multiyear sentence, his new company was a major player in the cable business in the United States.

Because I wanted a business to operate from, I retained the total ownership of Polar Distributors, Inc., which I eventually passed on my son Richard. I also kept the businesses and investments in which Henry Lewison and Irving Maturin were not participants. They were fortunate that Irving Kahn's Teleprompter Corporation continued to employ them to run the New York City master antenna system business, which serviced more than 400,000 people. The complexity of that business and their intimate knowledge of the customers and the system equipment made them the ideal managers for Teleprompter. I was just happy to be rid of them as partners without any confrontation or litigation.

I was now forty-two years old and decided to retire for a while and play golf. That would lead to a golf game that would kick off the series of inventions for which I would become most famous.

··14··

What Happened in Las Vegas

AT DUKE I HAD MET AN INSURANCE UNDERWRITER by the name of Ray Carlinsky, who was also on the Rice Diet but did not adhere to it. We played golf together at Duke University and became good friends. In the winter of 1966, Ray invited me to his home in Florida for a four-day weekend of golf. One of our foursome that weekend was Grant Sawyer, the former governor of Nevada who was now very active as the attorney representing the Nevada Gaming Commission. All he talked about during our casual golf games, and there was plenty of time to talk, was the skimming by underworld characters who controlled or owned most of the Las Vegas casinos, a situation he was unable to do anything about during his two terms as governor. Apparently the practice of siphoning off money before the tax collector could count it was cutting deeply into Nevada's revenues.

After listening to his skimming stories for three days, I said, Why don't you use a computer system to track and control each casino transaction the way large retail stores are doing? He asked where he could get such a system. My answer was that it did not exist, that it would have to be custom designed for the task, and that it would be a major undertaking, with the software being the largest part of the job. If properly funded, I estimated that it would take nine to twelve months or more to design, build, and test the system. He wanted to know who could accomplish such a task. My firm answer was that there was no one more qualified or better suited than my partner Dr. Wang at Wang Labs and myself. That was the end of the conversation.

A few weeks later, while playing in a Pro-Am golf tournament in Bermuda, I received a late-night phone call from Grant Sawyer. He wanted me to come to Las Vegas to meet with the Gaming Commission, the FBI, and the IRS, and tell them all about my proposal for a Casino Computer System. He had already sent to my office a set of first-class plane tickets to Las Vegas. What he did not know, and I didn't tell him, is that I had never set foot in a casino.

Without telling anyone, I changed my reservation to the day before the scheduled meeting, and I spent that day and night going from one casino to another studying their operations. I realized that what I had proposed would be a major hardware and software undertaking and my off-the-cuff estimate of at least nine months was short for the time needed to accomplish this task. The morning came and I had until 1 p.m. to prepare my presentation for this group of VIPs. I made some sketches on a yellow pad and went to a sign painter who made hand-painted signs and did the lettering on the side of trucks. I selected three cardboard display boards that measured 30 by 40 inches on which to post the finished drawings. At about 11:30, I rolled up the drawings and left for the airport to pretend I was arriving on my originally scheduled flight. Outside the luggage pickup carousel was a limo driver holding up a sign with my name. He drove me to the Desert Inn and took me directly to a huge penthouse suite where an assortment of food and drinks had been set out for me on the dining room table.

About twenty people, only three of them women, attended the meeting at the Gaming Commission's offices in downtown Las Vegas. Grant Sawyer gave me a big greeting and then introduced me to a number of VIPs in the room. I set up my three charts on a tall tripod in the corner at the front of the room and proceeded to explain the design of my system. I laid out the hardware and software components of the system, which included our development of something called a digital computer, which was the cheapest, quickest, and easiest way to accomplish the task at hand. In order to design the system properly and emulate every procedure and control that exists in a casino, I told them that I would need to have access to at least two casinos, both their operations and their books. I then opened the meeting to questions, which went on for over an hour. The committee then introduced me to Moe Dalitz, the chairman of the Hotel Owners Association, who would be my host during my stay in Las Vegas. We were all scheduled to meet again the next afternoon at 2 p.m., which would give the committee all morning to decide how to proceed.

I went back to the Desert Inn with Moe, who invited me to dinner with him that night. Promptly at 8 p.m. Moe took me across the street to the Silver Slipper, which he also owned, for dinner and a show. When we arrived, there was a huge showroom with at least a thousand people jammed together like sardines. Moe took me to a private table at the front of the stage that had about four feet of space around it. As soon as we sat down the orchestra started to play and out of the 40-foot ceiling came twelve large birdcages, each containing a gorgeous, almost naked woman. As the cages descended, at least four or five white birds flew out of each cage and into a larger one on the stage.

Unfortunately, on the way, one of the birds dropped a load directly on my toupee. When I removed my toupee, Moe handed it to a waiter to clean while we had our dinner and watched the show. The women on the stage stood within a few inches of where we sat; they were unbelievably beautiful, each one well endowed, tall, thin, and better looking than any other women I had ever seen in my life. At the end of the show, Moe asked if I liked any of them, and I quickly said that I liked all of them! He said that he could not do, but I could have any two I wanted that night.

The next morning, having gotten almost no sleep, I joined Moe at 7 a.m. for nine holes of golf and breakfast. Then at 2 p.m. I appeared at the Gaming Commission offices where Grant Sawyer immediately directed me to a conference room just for the two of us. He said that everyone had agreed to go ahead with the Casino Computer System but that funding this project, with all the government controls, restructurings, and procedures would require a great deal of time. That's why he was sitting with me here in a non-official capacity to discuss this dilemma. After thinking about this for a couple of minutes, I asked him if I could have a private room to call Dr. Wang. Grant quickly handed me a phone and left the room saying, "Get me when you're finished."

In my conversation with Dr. Wang, I said I would fund this new company, to be called Centronics, if we jointly developed this digital computer and divided up its use: I would have all rights to it as a computer system for casinos, and Wang would have all rights to the computer system for business applications. He agreed and with that I found Grant Sawyer and told him that if I could get the complete cooperation of the Gaming Control Board and the Hotel Owners Association, particularly Moe Dalitz, I would be willing to undertake the financing of this extremely complex system. It would take a substantial investment and I would probably need to do an Initial Public Offering, or IPO, to raise the funds needed. But in the meantime I would begin, and I would finance the company personally.

Grant told me that the Gaming Control Board would be more than willing to accept these conditions, and Moe Dalitz had offered the total cooperation of his five casinos in this undertaking and would recommend that all the members of the Hotel Owners Association do the same, because they all wanted the FBI, IRS, and Gaming Control Board off their backs. And so the deal was done. Our casino control system was under way.

When I first started to study the casino operations for the purpose of developing the casino computer system, I stayed in a luxurious penthouse apartment at the Desert Inn, and each morning I would play nine holes of golf and have breakfast with Moe and Allard Rowan, Moe's partner and attorney. I learned a lot about Las Vegas and the gambling business during those games. Then, from about three in the afternoon until four or five o'clock in the morning, I would study the gambling operations in the casino.

One day a couple of weeks after I arrived at the Desert Inn, Moe told me that I had to give up my magnificent penthouse suite and move to a suite on a lower floor because a VIP would soon be occupying the entire penthouse floor. Of course, I immediately did as he requested, as I was his guest in the hotel and paid for nothing. About three nights later, at 4:20 in the morning, an ambulance drove up to the front door, and two attendants cheerfully removed a man on a stretcher and wheeled him into the hotel and onto a special elevator that only serviced the penthouse floor.

I later found out that it was Howard Hughes who had taken up residence on the then totally isolated penthouse floor of the Desert Inn. I also found out that when the ambulance arrived to deliver Mr. Hughes to the hotel, he was not the man on the stretcher but one of the two men holding the stretcher. He went to great lengths to avoid being identified.

The problem was that Howard Hughes occupied what was called "the trading house floor," which was very special and used only for the exceptionally high rollers who came to the Desert Inn. So once the busy season started, Moe was under a great deal of pressure from some high rollers who came to his hotel and wanted to stay in one of these special suites on the penthouse floor. Moe had no choice but to ask that Mr. Hughes go to one of his other hotels that had accommodations available for him. But Hughes refused to leave the hotel, and to avoid further conflict Hughes bought the Desert Inn in early 1967. That's how, one by one, Hughes came to purchase seven casinos in Las Vegas.

BEING IN LAS VEGAS, I caught the casino bug, but my big opportunity to do something about it came from an unexpected direction, a good friend named Sam Lang who lived near us in Roslyn on Long Island. Our wives played cards and occasionally we would have dinner together or do something socially that involved our children, who were of the same age. I never knew what business Sam was in, but it seemed strange to me that he never appeared to go to work on a daily basis. I later found out that he had a service for professional photographers. His partner ran the business, and it was apparently very lucrative. I also found out that he was having an affair with his German housekeeper. Any night that he wanted to be with her, he would put a sleeping pill into his wife's evening cup of tea, and when she was asleep, he would sneak downstairs to the basement and have his way with his young, good-looking, and willing housekeeper.

My stake in the Bonanza Hotel and Casino (1968) provided an education on the way Las Vegas works.

One day Sam asked me if I wanted to invest in a casino hotel, called the Bonanza Hotel and Casino, that the New York garage king Larry Wolf wanted to build and run. We flew out to Las Vegas together, and when we arrived, a limousine was waiting to take us to Caesars Palace, a magnificent, comparatively new hotel on what is known in Las Vegas as the Strip. At that time there were two principal sections of Las Vegas. There was the older, downtown area, which had some beautiful new high-rise casino hotels, and there was the newer, more luxurious part of Las Vegas called the Strip, which catered to the high rollers. These were people who would take what are known as junkets; they were guests of the hotel who arrived from the East Coast on chartered flights together with more than a hundred other high rollers and were given the royal treatment. This included what was known as Room, Food, and Beverage, meaning that everything was free. In most cases the casinos' earnings from the gambling by these high rollers were more than adequate compensation for the cost of these freebies. Some people managed to successfully scam the system by appearing to be high rollers in order to get a free, all-expense-paid trip to Las Vegas.

Apparently whoever made the reservation for us told the casino that we were rich New York City investors coming for a few days of good times and gambling. When we arrived, we found ourselves guests of the hotel, each with a $25,000 line of credit. We were then given a beautiful two-bedroom suite, told that we had dinner and show reservations for 6 p.m., and, if we wished, they could provide us with two beautiful girls to keep us company during our stay.

The next morning Larry Wolf and his gorgeous wife, Rhoda, joined us for a luxurious breakfast in the huge living room–dining room section of our suite. After breakfast Larry rolled out a set of drawings and various sketches of the proposed Bonanza Hotel and Casino, which would take the place of a small, sixty-five-room, one-story motel that sat diagonally across the street from Caesars Palace. On the third corner stood Bugsy Siegel's original Flamingo Hotel, the first luxury hotel on the Strip. And on the fourth corner was the very luxurious Dunes Hotel, famous for its junkets and high roller treatment; behind it was an incredible golf course. The location just couldn't be beat.

Larry Wolf had negotiated an unbelievable deal with the owner of this sixty-five-room motel. He had guaranteed to lease the facility from him for 99 years for the amount of income he was currently receiving for operating it as a motel, adjusted each year to compensate for inflation. The owner, who was living in a room with a small kitchen behind the motel's small office, would have a free apartment in the new hotel and full hotel service as long as he lived.

The plan presented to us made a lot of sense and delivered a complete casino hotel at a fraction of the cost of any other to date. I decided to invest $250,000 and became a 2.5 percent owner of the Bonanza Hotel and Casino. Like every owner of a casino, I had to be licensed by Nevada Gaming Commission, which requires a very comprehensive application as well as a subsequent FBI investigation of the investor and where the money he is putting up comes from. All this went rather smoothly and we had a gala grand opening in which all the investors brought their families for a free weekend, which almost completely filled up the sixty-five hotel rooms, now spruced up with new carpet and furniture. The celebration included the presentation of a gold-engraved plate to each of the investors during a special dinner at the luxurious Bordello Room Restaurant overlooking the casino.

After the opening, business seemed to be doing quite well. The casino was full of people almost all the time, thanks largely to an old-time junket organizer who was in charge of bringing in twenty-five to fifty high rollers each week for a free weekend. Unfortunately, non–high rollers accounted for more than half the attendees because ours was a new casino without controls to sort these people out. Additionally, most of the investors sent friends on the junkets as high rollers, but who were not—imposing a cost to the casino that was not justified. As a result the investors held a secret meeting in New York, which was also attended by an investigator who was brought to the meeting by one of the investors. We decided to hire him for one month after which he would report back to us.

The news he brought back a month later was not good. He reported that we were being ripped off by the junketer and that the casino operation had so many holes in it that it would take an inside man to find out exactly what was going on. The cost he quoted us for hiring an inside man was outrageous, so we elected instead to send someone from our group and have that person stay there for a month, then someone else would go for another month, and so on, until we had a handle on the Bonanza's affairs. Since no one volunteered to be first, I suggested that Sam Lang, who had no day-to-day business to run and knew Larry Wolf better than of any of us, should be first.

Sam agreed and was off to the Bonanza the next afternoon, thinking that it would be a fun month in Las Vegas paid for by the investors. No one heard a word from Sam until two weeks into his trip, when I received a frantic phone call saying that I should come to Las Vegas on the next plane. He needed help but could not say why over the phone. When I arrived in Las Vegas, he met me at the airport, and in the car I asked him what was going on. He stopped the car next to an empty parking lot and needed to compose himself before launching into what so alarmed him. It seemed that almost everything at the casino hotel was being given away free. Dozens of people were apparently authorized to give away the complimentary shows, meals, and rooms with no controls and no real policy that the freebies should be tied to gambling. The winnings of the casino were supposed pay for all this. The problem was that the casino was not winning but losing money. The third shift had lost money every night since opening day and no one could explain why.

To find out, I spent eight all-night sessions in the casino, watching and talking to every person I could from our casino, as well as employees of other casinos, tourists, and some very strange-looking people who hung around Las Vegas. I learned a great deal about this business in comparatively little time. There was no doubt in my mind that we were being ripped off from the inside as well as the outside. It was well known around town that we were an easy mark because we had no connections. I discovered that there was no muscle on the inside to provide protection. It seems as though Larry Wolf had had a meeting with some gangster VIP before the casino opened, and the outcome of the meeting was a big, loud argument, after which the man stalked out in a rage, never to be seen again. I also heard a rumor that Larry Wolf was skimming cash from the casino every day; one person told me that he was taking $10,000 a night with an extra set of chips that only he knew about.

We now realized what a corrupt hotel and casino industry this was. Back in New York, our group of investors held a meeting in which I was asked to accept the full power to represent the 49 percent share that we, as a group, owned, and go to Las Vegas and take over the operation so we could stay alive long enough to sell the Bonanza and get out of the business. In the meantime we learned that Larry had needed working capital to keep the casino open. He had gone to a loan shark from Brooklyn to borrow $200,000, which was enough to keep the business open for about four weeks at the present cash-burn rate. My recommendation was that we should refuse to guarantee the money from the loan shark from Brooklyn, and confront Larry and demand that he give us the voting power of his stock so that we could stay open long enough to sell the place. It took a threat to turn over the information we had to the FBI, the IRS, and the Nevada Gaming Commission to get Larry to agree.

During this period, I spoke several times to Moe Dalitz and told him what was happening at the Bonanza. He said that our casino hotel, with its mere sixty-five rooms, would never survive; it was a money pit, but the land it sat on did have substantial value. He advised me to put up the money needed to stay afloat until a major hotel developer came along to build a 1,000- to 2,000-room hotel on the site. I valued Moe's advice and proposed to the investors that I take over the operation and give the hotel a $500,000 loan secured by a mortgage on the land and buildings, which was second only to the 99-year lease from the motel's former owner. I would then try to sell the business as quickly as possible.

What I did not tell the investors was that Moe wanted to meet Larry as soon as I got back to Las Vegas. When we arrived for the meeting at the Desert Inn, Allard Rowan, the attorney who was Moe's partner, greeted us. While waiting for Moe to show up, I told Larry that the investors had given me the authority to represent their share of the business and that they had sent me here to protect their investment. When Moe finally arrived, Larry put his hand out to shake Moe's hand, but Moe walked right past him, saying abruptly "Sit down!" Moe then told Larry that what he had done (and not done) at the Bonanza had caused problems for everyone in town. He said that people knew a lot more about what he had been up to than he was aware, and strongly recommended that he work out a departure plan with me that would get him out of the Bonanza — and Las Vegas — as quickly as possible. Moe was in the room for maybe a total of five minutes before he just got up and walked out without saying another word.

Larry was speechless. He knew, of course, that Moe was the most powerful man in Las Vegas and feared the consequences of not doing what Moe suggested. In the car on the way back to the Bonanza I told Larry that he had fooled no one, and that Moe had very detailed information of what had been going on both inside and outside the Bonanza. I told him it was now time for him to get out to stop the bleeding. I wanted him to give me the voting rights on his shares and stay around and help me make the transition to run and sell the Bonanza as quickly as possible. Starting the next day, I would be making all the decisions, the pit bosses would be on their way out, and there would be a new casino manager, courtesy of Moe.

Later, during a four-hour meeting with Larry and his wife, Rhoda, Larry agreed to everything. My group of investors would get 100 percent of their money back on their 49 percent, Larry could stay in town but not work in any casino, and his wife could continue to build her casino (without hotel)—all provided that everything at the Bonanza went as planned and it was sold within four months.

·· . 15.· ·

Adventures in Puerto Rico

IN THE COURSE OF MY ACTIVITIES in Las Vegas, I developed a
close personal and business relationship with Moe Dalitz, one
of the major figures who helped shape Las Vegas in the twentieth century. Moe was known as a bootlegger, racketeer, and all-
around bad guy, but based on my experiences with him, I
found him to be an incredible businessman and a very decent
friend. He extended himself far beyond what could be
expected to assist me in all of my business endeavors, as well as
give me investment advice about Las Vegas real estate, from
which I was able to profit handsomely. Without my knowledge,
Moe also gave me what he called his blessings during my time
running the Bonanza. Years later I found out that this consisted
of the protection of Moe Dalitz as though he were at my side
during any of my dealings in the casino industry. In subsequent
years this affiliation assisted me in my casino computer system,
real estate investments in Las Vegas, and slot machine manufacturing businesses. Moe Dalitz was a true gentlemen and I
am honored to have had him as a friend.

Of course, Moe's help was not entirely altruistic. It also
served him well, as he had been harassed by three government
agencies: the FBI, IRS, and the Nevada Gaming Commission.
They had tapped his phones, bugged his office and home, and

had people follow him everywhere. He was now cooperating with the authorities and helping me in developing the casino computer system.

At the same time, I was helping run the Bonanza and enjoying it because I had the advice of Moe's people whenever I needed it, and I needed it frequently. We only offered comps (complimentary room, food, and beverages) to real gamblers who gave the casino enough play to justify the freebies they received. We kept out the known casino scam experts and were able to spot the new ones. We also had to get rid of the insiders whose honesty was in question. Moe's people were invaluable in that respect. It turns out that everyone in the trade knew Larry's food and beverage manager as "Ten Percent" Dubensky. Everyone but Larry, that is, or if he did know, he didn't care.

Things were finally well under control at the Bonanza. We were showing a profit, and before long, a Wall Street firm, knowing that the place was up for sale, approached us with a client who was interested in purchasing the Bonanza. The client was said to be a successful company listed on the American Stock Exchange. But when I met the principals, they turned out to be typical New York garment center wise guys who had been going on junkets to the Dunes for years. I thought their desire to purchase the Bonanza just played to their egos and was a way to puff up the price of their company stock, which had no Wall Street glamour.

We argued over numerous meaningless points but finally made a deal for $10 million in cash and $14 million in restricted stock, for a total of $24 million, only subject to the Gaming Commission's license being granted, but with a $200,000 non-refundable deposit, which certainly helped our cash position. I let stand my mortgage on the property, which was at two points over prime, to be assumed by the seller, since I had been told that the new owners would probably fail and I would get the property back. About two months later they appeared before the Gaming Board and a few days later they were licensed, but it was a difficult deal to close because they did not understand how this industry worked. We structured the split of the proceeds among the investors so that Larry got his 51 percent of the $24 million, all in restricted stock, and we got the $10 million in cash plus any stock that was left. I also received the $250,000 I had invested plus $50,000 in stock, which would probably not be worth anything after the one-year restriction on selling the stock.

The company that bought the Bonanza lasted a year. While they were smart enough to keep our new casino management and dealers, they did not have the understanding that we had secured from Moe. They experienced the same problems we had had during Larry Wolf's management; they were giving almost everything away free, getting a great deal of action at the casino, but consistently losing at the tables instead of winning to pay off all of their expenses. They were too busy having fun and comping their friends and customers to free time at the casino, and they didn't have the financial resources to cover their losses. The company went bankrupt, and in bankruptcy court I was able to foreclose on my mortgage.

With the hotel and casino closed, I was desperate to do something quickly. A real estate agent told me that Kirk Kerkorian was looking for a site to put up his 1,200-room, MGM Grand Hotel and Casino. If Kerkorian bought the land behind the Bonanza, my site would be an ideal location for the MGM. But Kerkorian did not want to buy that additional land until he had the Bonanza. He didn't want to put me in a position that would allow me to demand an exorbitant price for the Bonanza. He was right, of course. We immediately started to negotiate, but we still had a problem with the original owner of the motel, with whom we had a 99-year lease and a promise to provide him with a place to live until he died. That obligation went along with the land, which substantially reduced the value of the land if the intent was to demolish the facilities and build a large hotel. I figured that if I could negotiate a deal with the prior owner before I sold to Kerkorian, I could get a lot more for the Bonanza than leaving that negotiation up to them.

Unfortunately, when I contacted the motel's prior owner, I learned that Kerkorian had already made a deal with him. That meant I couldn't get the price I was looking for, but I made the best deal I could with Kerkorian given the circumstances. I was just happy that the Bonanza fiasco was over. I could now refocus my attention on the casino computer system, the very enterprise that brought me to Las Vegas in the first place.

THE MINT HOTEL IN DOWNTOWN Las Vegas had the casino with the most transactions in all of Vegas, since the players were for the most part small betters. With the help of Moe Dalitz, I signed a deal with the manager of the Mint Hotel-Casino, a man named Bill Bennett, to install our first experimental Casino Computer System. We started the very complex installation by chopping channels in the floor to install a conduit with all of the wires that would connect the computer, at a central point, with each table, where a small input device would be installed. The technical problems were numerous, particularly regarding the software. Many changes could be made on the job almost immediately, but equipment modifications had to go back East to Wang Labs and took more time to complete.

The casino computer system we were installing would keep a constant check on what was going on at each table, controlling all the cash, chip, and credit transactions. Skimming occurred because no one had any idea how much money was going into the cash box. Someone would buy $200 worth of chips, for example, and receive $500 worth of chips. But with the casino computer system in place, when someone bought $200 worth of chips, the dealer or cashier had to enter, via the keyboard, that $200 was going into the cash box. In addition, the casino system kept track of the chips in the chip trays. Through a slit in the bottom of the tray, the system could scan the dollar value of all the chips in the trays, as chips of different value were coded differently. So when the cashier punched in $200, the computer watched that only $200 in chips was taken from the tray. This computerized "cash register" would also continually print a tape showing the nature and amount of each transaction, the table number, and the dealer's identity, and at any time during the day the computer could report the casino's current win or loss in dollars.

Our installation at the Mint Hotel was done quickly and became the talk of the town. Bill Bennett and I were on the front cover of a local Las Vegas magazine called *Follow Me*. The photo showed me standing at the blackjack table of his casino, pushing the buttons of the small computer entry terminal. Inside the magazine was a two-page article with numerous photos that showed our men at various stages of the installation. When the system was completed and the casino put it into full operation, the casino's percentage of the win changed from the usual 19 percent of the cash received to 21 percent, which was an enormous difference and a clear indication that the casino badly needed this system. The increased profits were so substantial that the cost of the system, which we rented for $65,000 a month, was insignificant.

FOLLOW ME
TO LAS VEGAS
MAGAZINE

Volume 3 • No. 4   November 1967 60c

MINT HOTEL PIONEERS — Robert Howard, right, president of Centronic Data Inc., demonstrates new electronic cash register installation to Wm. Bennett, vice president and general manager of The Mint Hotel-Casino. The Nevada Gaming Commission has approved a "trial installation" at the downtown casino.   See Page 4

On the cover of the November 1967 issue of *Follow Me to Las Vegas Magazine*: I'm demonstrating my new casino computer system to Bill Bennett, the general manager of the Mint Hotel-Casino.

After two weeks of operation, I picked up Cliff Perlman, the chairman of Caesars Palace, and we drove to the Mint Hotel during the busiest time of the evening. After spending about an hour together, we went back to his spectacular office at Caesars Palace and immediately started discussions. He wanted ownership of a substantial block of shares in Centronics and I wanted to install our casino computer system in Caesars Palace, the most prestigious casino in all of Nevada. After trying to think of ways to meet both of our objectives, I mentioned the fact that I had an option on the 600,000 shares owned by Sam Lang, who had worked with me on the casino computer system at the beginning but was no longer active in the company. Even though I could buy the stock back from Lang at half the price of the IPO (the stock price was already four times that option price), for the best interests of the company I offered the 600,000 share option to Cliff Perlman in exchange for a five-year, noncancelable contract for our casino computer system at $65,000 a month. He would not agree to that, but did agree to install our casino system for a minimum of one year, and if the contract were canceled for any reason, he would return to the company, without charge, 300,000 of the 600,000 shares that he would purchase from Sam Lang.

This deal went through but complications arose just a few months later. Moe wanted us to move our operation to Puerto Rico and not have any installations in Las Vegas for at least two years, and we complied with his request. We had never considered the possibility of Centronics canceling the contract with Caesars, but the wording in our agreement could be interpreted either way. Of course, this marked the end of my personal relationship with Cliff Perlman, but "Business is business," as my grandfather would say. This also ended our casino computer system business in Las Vegas.

Moe had a good reason for wanting my casino system out of Las Vegas and he didn't hesitate to tell me why. I had a marvelous understanding with Moe Dalitz; we always spoke honestly with each other, never needing to distort any of the facts. He told me quite bluntly he was looking to sell his casinos and other investments in Las Vegas and get out of town because he could no longer cope with the tension created by all of the government agencies looking to put him in jail for skimming casino profits. But while he might have done just that in the past, he was now doing exactly the opposite—putting money into the casinos to show additional winnings and profits. He hoped that by showing high profits, a buyer would pay a higher price for his casinos. But there was a problem. Putting my casino system into his casinos would prevent him from inflating the value of his casinos in this way.

With that in mind Moe asked me to take my casino system to Puerto Rico and stay out of Las Vegas for at least the next two years, just enough time for him to sell his casinos. He said that if I would do this for him, he would see to it that all or most of the casinos in Puerto Rico would quickly sign up to install our casino computer systems and pay the $65,000 a month in rental fees. Based on the normal formulas for leasing computer equipment at that time and based on our cost for the equipment, the rental price should have been about $6,000 a month, including maintenance. Making ten times that amount would certainly put my company in a very profitable situation.

I immediately got on a plane and went to Puerto Rico where I had a meeting with Lou Puro, the owner of two newly constructed casinos, the El San Juan and the brand-new El Conquistador. Apparently Moe had spoken to Lou, and signing him up for our casino computer system was probably the easiest sale I have ever made in my entire life. I went directly back to Las Vegas and quickly held a press conference announcing our contract with two casinos in Puerto Rico and explained why it was easier and better for us to do our initial installations there. Since the casinos in Puerto Rico were only open eight hours a day and closed for sixteen, we could install and test the casino computer system during the sixteen hours the casino was closed without in any way disrupting their normal operations during the hours that the casino was open.

The El San Juan was the first to have our casino computer system installed. About one hundred yards from the casino, along the beach on the other side of the Americana Hotel Casino, were some small furnished apartments to rent. Since I would be spending a good bit of time in Puerto Rico during the installation of these systems—along with Sam Lang, who would be helping me on this venture—we decided to rent one of these apartments. A day or two after we moved in, we discovered that most of the apartments were being rented by the gorgeous showgirls who were appearing in the French Extravaganza topless show that was a permanent fixture at the Americana Hotel.

The apartment complex had a pool on the front side of the building and 150 feet of magnificent white sand beach in the back. These showgirls had nothing to do during the day except enjoy the beach or the pool since they only worked for a few hours around dinnertime. Sam and I became friendly with a number of them, as it hardly ever took more than a few hours each day for us to review with our foreman and installation employees exactly what they had completed the day before and what they needed to do that day. Then we were free to frolic with the girls on the beach or at the pool in the afternoon.

Most evenings we would spend in the casino getting friendly with the employees, particularly the casino manager whose name was Charlie Garcia, a very good-looking young man with jet black hair who had an unbelievably gorgeous Spanish girl-friend. When we first came to Puerto Rico, Centronics was just going public at $5 a share; I made a gift of some shares to four of the key employees of the El San Juan, including Charlie Garcia.

Our $65,000 a month rental charge for this system proved to be a substantial bargain for the casinos. The casino's "hold," or the dollar amount of cash winnings taken in by the casino each day, was normally about 19 percent. But, as with the Mint Hotel in Las Vegas, their hold increased to 21 percent once our system was installed. This additional win came as a result of the much stricter controls and monitoring of every table and every dealer, which our system provided. As a result, we had some very happy casino operators, and the rest of the casinos in Puerto Rico were now anxious to have our system installed as well.

Some months later four casinos had installed our system. Wall Street analysts took note of our unusually high profits and as a result our stock was selling for more than ten times the original offering price. Charlie Garcia told me that he would like to leave the casino manager's position and open a restaurant of his own. If the Centronics stock doubled in value, he would have enough money to open his own business. I jokingly asked him, if I do that for you, what you are going to do for me? His answer was right to the point: he said if his stock sold for twice the amount that it was at that day, he would treat me to a one-night stay with his girlfriend; he knew I had an eye for her. He was right. I quickly shook his hand and said that we had a deal.

About a year and a half later someone told me that Charlie had left his job as casino manager and had opened the restaurant of his dreams, which was very successful. On my next visit to Puerto Rico, I arranged to see Charlie's new restaurant and have dinner with him. He had a big smile on his face when greeted me, gave me a hug, and thanked me for making this all possible for him. I said that I had come to Puerto Rico to collect on his promise. At that point his face blanched because he had probably forgotten about our deal. He had since married his girlfriend and she was now seven months pregnant. That meant I couldn't collect. During the course of the conversation his wife came in to greet me, and even though she was pregnant, she was still gorgeous. I know better now not to count my sheep before they get into the pen.

ONE DAY LONG AFTER THE BONANZA AFFAIR, Sam Lang came to me with another business proposal. He wanted me to invest fifty-fifty with him in a six-story garage on the East Side of Manhattan, on which he had an option to convert to an office building. He needed two of the floors to expand his business. The value of the offices per square foot would be at least four to five times their value as a garage. The other four floors needed to be rented to someone who would undertake some major alterations, including the huge front-end cost for plumbing, electricity, and all the walls and partitions. I am a risk taker, but this was too big of a risk for me to undertake. Besides, the garage was owned by Larry Wolf, and after the Bonanza affair, Wolf was the last person in the world I wanted to deal with again.

That proved to be a big mistake. The profit from this venture was enormous, because it turned a great deal of very cheap space into very expensive space in a very desirable neighborhood that commanded the highest rents per square foot in New York City. Ultimately, Sam made a great deal of money by selling his business as well as this building.

I was about to make a great deal of money myself—but in an entirely new industry.

··16··

From Slots to Dots

CENTRONICS WAS ORIGINALLY part of Wang Laboratories, during which Dr. An Wang and I jointly developed the casino computer system. Wang Laboratories had its origins back in the early 1950s when An Wang started an unincorporated research and development company that specialized in electronics and digital equipment. Originally Wang had no plans to develop and build computers. He had left his native China in 1945 to study applied physics at Harvard University, where he earned his doctorate in 1948. After graduation Wang did postdoctoral work at Harvard's Computational Laboratory, where he invented the magnetic pulse core memory, which was an early form of random access computer memory that would become a standard component of large analog computers for the next quarter of a century. When Harvard announced in 1951 that it was suspending computer research, Wang left the university. With no contracts and no orders, he started Wang Laboratories later that year, with only $600 in capital. The company's early focus was the development of specialized electronic equipment that would utilize Wang's magnetic core memory.

My own long business relationship with Dr. Wang began in 1955, when I brought a barrel full of military-rejected transistors to his office to see if they were good enough to be used in cable and other commercial equipment. In 1961, with the introduction of the first digital computer by the Digital Equipment Corp. (DEC), Wang and I felt that digital was the future of the computer business. Wang decided to build a digital computer that would satisfy the needs of Wang Labs and our contemplated casino computer system.

Though An Wang and I were the principal owners of Centronics, as a result of our working together on the casino system, Moe Dalitz did have a 10 percent stake in the company. Moe did not need to invest any money for this ownership, as his assistance and the fact that he was associated with our company was priceless. He was such a gentleman that when he asked me to leave Las Vegas and move my casino computer operation to Puerto Rico, I agreed to do it immediately and he returned his 10 percent ownership of Centronics to me as a token of his appreciation.

Once I decided that Centronics would become an independent company, I assigned Prentice Robinson, who had run Centronics when it was part of Wang, the task of finding a place for the seven people who were coming with me from Wang Labs to produce the casino computer system. It was Robinson's decision to locate Centronics in Hudson, New Hampshire, where he and his family lived. For several years he had been trying to get Dr. Wang to agree to locate the expansion of Wang Labs in southern New Hampshire rather than Massachusetts because of the huge tax advantages available in New Hampshire and the abundance of skilled technical people who would work for salaries far lower than workers in Massachusetts.

On Library Street in Hudson, New Hampshire, was a fifty-year-old wooden house whose main floor had been converted to law offices. The second floor, which was unoccupied at the time, had originally consisted of one large bedroom and three small ones. We rented this space and quickly put some benches and stools into two of the rooms. Since we used soldering irons in our work, the electrical supply in the building was insufficient, so we hired an electrician to bring new power into the building and run it up to the four rooms on the second floor. The smallest bedroom was set up for our files and the last one we set up as an office with three desks, one for Prentice Robinson, one for Ann Morrison, who was our do-everything woman, and one for myself.

We immediately started producing our casino systems under contract for delivery and installation in the Puerto Rican casinos. But our second-floor space barely gave the eight of us enough room to work efficiently. Fortunately there was some unused space in the attic, where we installed a floor, and used it as a storage space for inventory and works in progress. We were now an operating company with orders, backlog, and a functioning factory.

In starting Centronics, we had a great deal of engineering talent but needed a businessman on the inside to control expenditures. As a result I hired Fred Jacobs, who had been my partner in Cool Heat Corp., as my executive vice-president as well as the CFO even though his Ph.D. was in engineering, because he had a good understanding of how to financially control a business. For a number of years thereafter Fred Jacobs was the number two executive after Prentice Robinson, who was now the CEO of Centronics.

In 1968, Centronics became a public company, independent of Wang Laboratories. The full name of Centronics was the "Centronics Data Computer Corp." because at the time of the IPO, if the word "data" or "computer" was part of a company's name, it was perceived to be a very hot stock. At this time the stock market would oversubscribe to almost every IPO of a computer-related start-up looking for initial financing. But the Centronics IPO was a lot more than that: we had a casino computer system in operation in Puerto Rico that was paying $65,000 a month rent, as well as a backlog of signed contracts for three additional casino systems. We had a factory in Hudson, New Hampshire, with seven employees and 700 square feet of factory space.

The public offering for Centronics was for 800,000 shares at $5 per share, which gave us almost $4 million cash in working capital. Since the IPO was substantially oversubscribed, we gave everyone only half of the amount of stock they had committed to take. On the first day of trading on the over-the-counter market, the stock increased to more than $7 a share. All of the initial stockholders were very pleased with their investment.

With the casino computer system selling well, we began working on the design of a new concept that I had for a slot machine—an electronic slot machine. Until then all slot machines utilized a very old and rather unreliable physical mechanism. The payouts were determined by combinations of symbols, such as cherries, on each of the three or four wheels of the slot machine. This combination limited the maximum payout to about 1,000 coins. So it was impossible to have the kind of huge jackpots that would attract more players. But in an electronic slot machine, you can program a computer using stepper motors, electric motors that can divide a full rotation into a large number of steps, to randomly select winning or losing symbols to have huge statistical odds with huge payouts, one million coins, and still maintain a percentage of win for the house. This would turn out to be a tremendous attraction for future players of slot machines even though their chances of winning would be greatly reduced.

Our all-electronic slot machine, which we began licensing under a separate company called Gamex Industries Inc. in the early 1970s, was another one of our innovative products that was a little ahead of its time. We struggled to gain the acceptance of the electronic slot machine by an industry that was very reluctant to accept changes. At the same time we rolled our casino computer system into Gamex as well. Now that Centronics was listed on the NYSE, I really needed to divest the company of all things gambling-related. I had decided that I didn't want to be in the gambling business anymore. Centronics was now in a product, marketing, and financial position to grow itself into becoming the principal manufacturer of a new and expanding worldwide business in the next few years. That business would be computer printers.

ONE OF THE MOST SIGNIFICANT inventions of my career grew out of a need we discovered during the installation of the casino computer system at the Mint Hotel. We needed a printer we could hook up to the system that could quickly produce multiple copy documentation of the transactions, as well as receipts. But the only choices available at the time were either a large, noisy, $25,000 line printer, which was not only far too expensive but also much too large to fit in the small space of the "pit" of the casinos, or a $2,000 teletype printer, which was far too slow, producing only 10 characters per second, and very unreliable. By necessity we chose the latter, but we really needed something that could print multiple copies at the rate of 150 to 200 characters per second.

We had to find another solution to the printer problem, one that was reliable and fast enough to keep up with the gamblers. Back in my workshop in New York City, I began by experimenting with ultrasonic sound waves. My original idea was to use sound waves, shot as if from a gun, to create small dots, which when completed would form letters and numbers. It would work in much the same manner as the thermal printer I had seen, which used heat to form the dots on special sensitive paper. But thermal technology was unacceptable for casino use because the information could not be stored on this special paper permanently. It would fade away with time or when exposed to warm temperatures. Besides, thermal printers weren't fast enough and didn't produce multiple copies either. So we ran some tests to see if we could produce dots on paper by shooting ultrasonic sound waves through a ribbon onto a multiple (four-copy) receipt. This idea wasted six weeks of valuable time proving that it could not work. It was a painful process.

My next idea was to develop a new kind of solenoid, an electromagnetic switch that converts energy into motion, that would be fast and powerful enough to create an impact dot through a ribbon onto a multiple copy paper form, as required in our casino computer system. Several tiny metal wires would sweep across the page and produce the dots that would form the alphanumeric characters. The wires would need to strike an inked ribbon with enough force to produce a series of dots onto all four copies of the multiple copy form used in our system. The wires needed to be driven by a very fast acting solenoid of no less than 1,000 strokes per second, which I quickly discovered did not exist. The challenge then became to improve the state-of-the-art of the solenoid, a technology that has been around for a hundred years, which meant that improving it would not be a simple task. This required doing research that included reading whatever I could find about the theory of solenoids as well as talking to some of the engineering experts in that field.

I learned that, electronically, solenoids could accept exceptionally fast signals and could drive the armature forward fast enough, but mechanically, the time required to retract it to be in a position to be fired again was the limiting factor to the speed of the solenoid. Once it was fired, how could I get it back fast enough? In studying the different kinds of springs that were in use, I came upon one called a torsion bar spring. I designed one that was about half an inch in diameter, looked like a cartwheel, and was particularly well suited for this application. The spring's tension would increase logarithmically with each incrementally small amount of movement. In this application I was limited to having approximately one-tenth of an inch of movement of the armature with the wires attached, the end of which would impact the ribbon though a guide, aligning all seven wires vertically. One spring went into each solenoid and there were seven solenoids in the printhead.

This spring design turned out to be the key to the invention that would eventually become known as the dot matrix printer. In it, a tiny bank of wires runs back and forth across the page and prints by impact, striking an ink-soaked cloth ribbon against the paper in letter-shaped patterns. The effect is similar to a fleet of skywriting planes. Because the letters produced by an impact printer are drawn from a matrix of dots, various fonts, languages, and simple graphics can be produced. And because the printing involves mechanical pressure, these printers can create carbon copies and carbonless copies.

The torsion bar spring performed better than my best expectations. It was fast enough to achieve 165 characters per second. In the rush to make this calculation, however, I made a mistake —the actual speed of the manufactured machines was 185 characters per second, yet even to this day, the Centronics matrix character printer is officially rated at 165 characters per second.

Once I had the printhead designed and functioning in a manner that satisfied the needs of our application, we installed it into a small adding machine mechanism to print alphanumeric characters for the first time. We then produced a hundred dot matrix printheads for alpha testing and achieved very acceptable results.

Now that I had a manufacturable solenoid that was working properly, I needed to work out the details to start producing the mechanism and the electronics in the printheads in volume in a reliable, cost-effective way. Centronics had the skill to design and build both the printheads and the electronics in production quantities efficiently. But we were not able to manufacture the printer mechanism itself and had to find someone to do it to our specifications with cost and quality requirements.

Again, a member of the Road Runners, the group of men I played golf with every weekend, came to the rescue. Max Hugel was the president of Brother International Corp., the exclusive distributor of Brother Ltd. of Nagoya, Japan. At that time, Brother was the largest producer of sewing machines in the world; they also produced huge quantities of typewriters each month. This seemed like the ideal company to produce our printer mechanisms. The problem was that it required the commitment of at least $5 to $8 million up front for the engineering, tooling, and production facilities. When I complained about my dilemma during a golf game with my Road Runner friends the next weekend, Max invited me to discuss the matter in his office on Monday morning.

After several hours of detailed conversation with Max and his partner, Roy Nakagowa, on Monday, Max concluded that we should pitch the idea in person to the chairman of Brother. We were off to Japan.

·..17..·

The Brother I Never Had

WHEN WE ARRIVED AT THE AIRPORT in Tokyo, we were greeted by three Brother executives who drove us to the train station, where we took a luxurious 120-mile-per-hour bullet train to Nagoya. We arrived an hour later to find two small limousines waiting to take us to the Brother corporate headquarters. There we were introduced to the executive vice-president, Mr. Shiyuiti Kawashima, and Mr. Masami Hanazono, who was the director of engineering. Mr. Hiromi Gungi, one of the greeters, would become the president of Brothers's worldwide distribution company twenty years later. After introductions and an exchange of business cards, we left in three cars for dinner at a small restaurant with a private room for the six of us. I had no idea what all the dishes were, but they were delicious. The main course was kobe beef; it was the best steak I ever had. We toasted at least ten times during the course of the meal. They all spoke broken English, but Max spoke perfect Japanese.

At breakfast Max and I had a strategy meeting in preparation for our meeting with the chairman of Brother. Max asked me to take out one of my business cards on which was printed my name as the chairman of the company and the logo in the center that was an artistic representation of the company's initials: CDC. Because of their limited English, Max said, they will all think I was the chairman of CDC, the Control Data Corp., rather than Centronics Data Computer, Inc. In the 1960s, Control Data Corp. built the fastest computers in the world. Max said that I should not correct them if they made this mistake; he would deal with it in Japanese. We talked about the fact that Brother was always looking for new products and industries to get into. They had just recently abandoned a very costly attempt to start manufacturing and selling very high quality pianos. This failure created a welcome opportunity for us; the timing and comparatively small cost of entry into this venture was ideal for Brother.

When we entered the meeting room, everyone was sitting around a huge conference table on which lay our small 20-character-wide calculator mechanism with the new printhead, some very crude unpackaged electronics, and a keyboard to show how alphanumeric characters could be printed by the printer. Herb Menhennett, one of my engineers, had come to Nagoya a day ahead of us, specifically to set up this demonstration unit and see to it that it worked. Next to the model we had a full-size mechanical drawing of the mechanism needed for our 80-column-wide product with sprocket feed tractors, which could accept forms of variable width.

After three pretty young women came in with cups of tea for everyone at the table, we demonstrated our prototype and printed through a ribbon some dot matrix alphanumeric characters on a roll of calculator paper. We then passed out these small pieces of paper to our audience. After about two hours of demonstrations and discussions, we were led to another conference room on the top floor of the building, where we met the chairman, Masayoshi Yasui, who was one of the two founding brothers of the company in 1932. We shook hands and exchanged business cards. Because Yasui did not speak a word of English, Max and the three other Japanese executives explained the situation to him. But apparently the decision to move ahead on this project had already been made.

A group of young women brought in tea and small cups of sake for toasting to our new business relationship. The chairman told Max that we should draft an agreement between our two companies. We shook hands and went back downstairs for lunch, which was followed by a tour of the Brother sewing machine and typewriter manufacturing facility. Later, at a dinner where bear paw soup was served, I immediately lost my appetite. The next morning we were back in Tokyo for our flight to New York. While sitting in first class, Max and I drafted the essential business terms for our attorneys to use as a guide in writing a ten-year manufacturing and supply agreement between our two companies.

THE PROTOTYPE DESIGN and construction period took approximately four months. Centronics engineer Herb Menhennett was stationed at Brother and assigned the difficult task of coordinating the effort. Brother was building the printer mechanism itself as Centronics prepared the electronics package, which included the power supply and a matrix printhead. Even though Herb was at Brother full-time, I still needed to travel to Nagoya once a week in the beginning to monitor the progress of the design, the selection of components, and the testing of the individual parts.

As a consequence, I became a frequent flyer on Pan Am flights to and from Japan. I liked having the three center seats available to stretch out and go to sleep, but they were not always available even though the flights were usually half empty. When I complained to my travel agent, she managed to reserve the center three seats in the last row for me, so that after

I had my dinner in first class, I could go to the back of the plane, stretch out, and go to sleep for the remainder of the fourteen-hour flight.

On one of these flights, I had my dinner, then set myself up in the center seats with four pillows stacked high at one end, so that I could rest my head on the armrest, and quickly fell sound asleep. A few hours later, I woke up and went to the bathroom. Much to my surprise, I saw in the mirror that my hairpiece was gone. I quickly went back to my center seats and searched for it, but to no avail. I then called one of the stewardesses to help me find my toupee. She then started laughing and said, "So that's what it was!"

It seems that a few hours before, one of the stewardesses must have brushed by my head in such a way that my toupee stuck to the back of her dress. As she wandered about the plane, the passengers who saw it started to laugh as she walked away from them. This went on for a half hour, until one of the other stewardesses saw it, put a napkin over it, and pulled it off her dress and put it into the garbage. After that, whenever I would fly with this crew, we would always have a good laugh, on me.

OUR GOAL WAS TO HAVE the printer ready for the largest trade show of the electronics industry, which occurred in Atlantic City each spring. We arranged to have a booth at that show, although due to our late entry, we were lucky to get a small booth in the far corner of the basement floor. We prepared the booth with just one large sign that read: "165 CPS—$2,400. OEM Price." Everyone in the industry knew what those initials meant: CPS stands for characters per second, and OEM stands for original equipment manufacturer.

In New Hampshire we designed, tested, and manufactured the power supply and electronics, which would fit into a cavity at the back of the printer that Brother would produce. After testing the components as best we could, I hand carried the electronics and a printhead to Japan to be installed in the first matrix printer prototype. After fitting everything together into the printer, we connected it to a computer, turned on the power, and waited to see it printing. It did not. There were several problems that Herb Menhennett and two electrical engineers at Brother spent several hours ironing out before we were ready to turn the machine on again. But when we did, it successfully printed several pages from the computer. Everyone involved in the project viewed this as a remarkable accomplishment.

Unfortunately we were now only forty-six hours from the start of the show in Atlantic City. In order to have this printer present for the opening of the show, it had to travel from Nagoya to Tokyo to New York City and then to Atlantic City. It was an almost impossible task but I decided to try to do it. We put our only working machine into a wooden box that measured 30 inches long and 24 inches wide, and 18 inches high, with a rope handle at either end. It weighed well over one hundred pounds and took two strong men to carry it. With help from the Brother people, Herb and I carried this box from the car to the bullet train and boarded the train quickly. We knew that this train was for passengers and hand baggage only. Once we boarded the train we quickly went to our seats, leaving the box in the area reserved for hand baggage. The conductor came and shouted to us in Japanese. Just as the Brother people explained to him that we spoke no Japanese, the doors closed and the train was on its way to Tokyo, the next stop. I told the Brother people to tell the conductor that I would take the box off the train as soon as we got to Tokyo; the conductor had no choice but to accept my apologies.

When we arrived in Tokyo, Herb and I carried the box to the taxi stand. We tried to put the box in the trunk of a taxi, but it was too big, so we tried to put it into the back seat of the car. When the taxi driver got out and started shouting at us in Japanese, I pulled out my wallet and gave him ¥10,000. He removed the back seat and helped us put the box in the back of his cab. We then followed his cab in another cab to the airport. I had only one hour before the Pan Am nonstop flight left for New York City. There was a long line at the check-in counter so Herb and I carried the box to the front of the line and put it down on the scale. We were able to do that because the first two people in line were Japanese, very courteous people, who said nothing about our jumping to the front of the line.

When we gave the Japanese Pan Am agent our first-class tickets with our passports, he looked at the box and said: "This is freight. It cannot go on this flight. You must go to the freight terminal."

I told him it wasn't freight; it was my luggage.

"But that's much too heavy to be luggage," he said. "What's in it?"

"It's filled with shoes," I replied.

He then said I had to pay an overweight charge, which I did gladly, and got on the plane. When we arrived in New York, Max Hugel was waiting with a large limousine to drive me directly to Atlantic City. Unbelievably, I arrived in Atlantic City with the printer at 7:30 p.m., with the show scheduled to start the next morning. We worked all night to set it up because when we unpacked the printer, it did not work. We stuck numerous print samples into the printer to look as though it had just printed, even though it wasn't working.

Although our exhibit was located in just about the worst possible location in the Exposition Center, there was a great deal of interest in our product. Ours was the most crowded booth in that part of the basement. In the course of the show, we discovered that we had the only product in the industry that had the desired price and performance specifications. We accepted orders for 52 Centronics Model 101 Dot Matrix Printers at $2,400 each. When customers asked how they could qualify for the OEM price, I responded that they needed to have $2,400.

With that, we were now off and running to becoming the largest computer printer manufacturer in the United States. It had taken just one year, from idea to finished product. The Centronics Model 101 Dot Matrix Printer was introduced in 1970, and the dot matrix printer would rule the printer world for nearly two decades, until it was replaced by the ink-jet printer in the 1990s. But dot matrix technology remains in use today in cash registers, ATMs, and many other point of sale terminals.

It's worth mentioning that the Model 101 Dot Matrix Printer included the first parallel interface for printers, an innovation that would prove to be enormously influential in its own right. The interface was developed by Dr. An Wang, Prentice Robinson, and myself at Wang Laboratories. When we decided on the detailed specifications for the interface, we were looking to establish a universal method of communicating in both directions with virtually any computer. Previously computer manufacturers had prevented others from attaching their peripheral devices to their computers by using a unique interface. We came to the conclusion that if we developed a very easy, simple interface and gave it free to the world, it might be accepted and used by everyone. Apparently the practice of creating unique interfaces was so resented by everyone in the computer industry that once IBM accepted our interface, seven other major companies immediately followed suit.

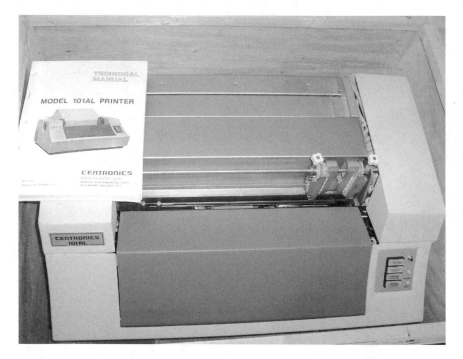

My enormously successful dot matrix printer, the Centronics Model 101 (above), in 1970, with a close-up of the printerhead (below)

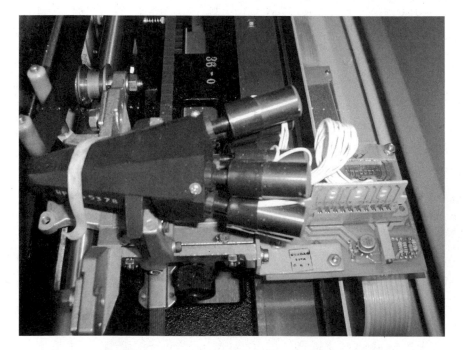

Why did we use the connector we ended up using? Because during the design stage, we became aware that Wang had a surplus stock of 200,000 Amphenol 36-pin micro ribbon connectors that were originally used for one of his early scientific calculators, so we specified that connector, even though it was really quite a bit larger than it needed to be for our purposes. The 36-pin Centronics Parallel Interface quickly became the de facto industry standard and was used in almost every computer manufactured in the world until the advent of the USB interface at the end of the twentieth century.

ONCE WE HAD THE Centronics Model 101 Dot Matrix Printer in hand we began a dialogue with "Snow White and the Seven Dwarfs"; "Snow White" was IBM, while "the Seven Dwarfs" were the other seven computer companies in existence at that time. When we demonstrated our printer to each of them, they came to the conclusion that alphanumeric characters composed of a series of dots were not sharp enough for a business system. Basically, the printer didn't give fully formed characters. If a dot was missing it could potentially change a word or a number. I agreed but argued that if a dot matrix printer were fast enough, cheap enough, and reliable enough, there would be an enormous market for the product. About this I would be proven quite correct.

During the first talks with IBM, they requested that some of their personnel be allowed to visit our manufacturing facility. I told them that I would be happy to do that if they would give me a reciprocal tour through their own printer facility, and they agreed. I spent the better part of a day visiting their printer manufacturing facility and found that only one engineer really knew and understood the small printer business. His name was Richard Williams. I offered Williams the position of vice-president of engineering of Centronics and he accepted. We spoke almost every day for the next twenty years or so, helping each other do a better job, until he retired as chairman of a subsequent company I founded named Presstek.

Although Snow White and the Seven Dwarfs had no interest in our printer, our appearance at the Atlantic City trade show had captured the attention of a distributor for Nixdorf, the largest computer company in Europe. The distributor ordered a printer and we shipped it to him in time for the next trade show, the largest in Europe, which would take place in Düsseldorf, Germany. Within an hour of the show's opening, Heinz Nixdorf, the founder and chairman of the company, personally came to the distributor's booth and saw how well our printer was running, making multiple copies. We were offering it at a very attractive price compared to the printer that Nixdorf was offering with the computers it manufactured. After spending about an hour watching the printer perform and listening to the comments of the customers, Nixdorf requested that I meet with him at the end of the day and join him for dinner.

After meetings with Nixdorf that afternoon, evening, and the following morning, we had a piece of paper that outlined a contractual arrangement for Nixdorf to purchase half of our total production for the next two years. As part of that agreement he would advance us $2 million so that we could go into production with hard tooling instead of the soft tooling that Brother had initially contemplated. Later that week, back in New York, I met with the Nixdorf attorney and my attorney to prepare the agreement, which also contained an additional investment of $6 million for 10 percent of the stock of our company. But his attorney made so many demands, guarantees, and personal encumbrances on my shares, that it made

This may be the only time I ever overlooked my Centronics printers.

the investment portion of the agreement impossible to consummate. Nevertheless we ended up with a very lucrative,
five-year OEM supply agreement with Nixdorf Computer,
who was by far our best customer for a number of years. Heinz
Nixdorf and I became good personal friends until he died of a
heart attack about a decade later.

Production at Brother was increasing at a substantial rate, while maintaining their marvelous quality, and it appeared as though our business plan, which called for the sale of 1,000 dot matrix printer mechanisms from Brother by the end of the third year, would be reached in half the time, and sales would grow exponentially after that. The revenue of Centronics in 1971 was $650,000; it then grew to $7 million in 1972, to $20 million in 1973, and to $42 million in 1974—quite a start for a small company with a public offering of $5 million. Seven years after our IPO at $5 a share, the shares had split twelve times, were worth more than $50 each, and paid 25 cents a share in dividends. That meant the original $5 shares were now worth $600 apiece.

AFTER FOUR VERY SUCCESSFUL YEARS at Centronics, Prentice Robinson, my Mr. Inside, decided that he wanted to leave his wife and two children and move to Alaska with his secretary. He said that the $20 million of stock that he owned, together with the several million dollars that he already received on the sale of some of his shares, was more money than he would ever want in his life. He was driven by a desire for a new, younger mate and a life in Alaska where he could spend his time salmon fishing, a sport he loved, whenever he wanted.

My analysis of his situation told me that this dream would not work out for Prentice. I thought the pair would quickly be bored of each other and Alaska, and that he would miss his two lovely children after being away from them for several months. I suggested that he go to Alaska and then, after six months, come back so we could make some permanent arrangement. Though I would continue his salary during those six months, I insisted that he and his girlfriend not speak to me or anyone else connected with the company about either business or personal matters during the six-month period. We shook hands and he left without a word to another person in the company.

I was sure that he would return to his job, but I was wrong. Exactly six months later he came into my office and said that he had decided to stay in Alaska and wanted to resign all of his positions in the company. He appreciated my generosity and said the six-month salary that he had received was more than sufficient as termination pay. With that, he said good-bye.

With the departure of Robinson, I now had to run the day-to-day operations of the company, so I decided to find a permanent home in New Hampshire. I had been staying in a small suite that cost me $10 a night at the Nashua Country Club, where I was a member. I decided to build a house on a nearby lake called Cobbits Pond, where boating, swimming, and fishing were permitted. The lake was eight miles long and three miles wide, with small vacation homes all around the perimeter. I bought a magnificent piece of property that was owned by the only remaining member of the family who originally owned the entire lake more than 150 years before. The property included a peninsula that jutted out into the lake with a small sand beach on the shoreline.

It was now January 1971, and the land was bought, the architect was chosen, and the excavation for construction had started on our house on the lake. A few months later when the foundation was in place and the structure was going up, my son Larry moved to New Hampshire, the end point of what can only be called a long, strange trip.

$\cdot\cdot\cdot18\cdot\cdot\cdot$

Children and Other Investments

MY SON LARRY HAD GRADUATED from high school as a star of the basketball team, then went to college at The George Washington University in Washington, D.C., more to play basketball than to get an education. But just a few months after the start of his first semester, someone accidentally stuck a finger into his left eye while he was playing basketball. The injury was severe and he was devastated when doctors told him that he could no longer play competitive basketball. The news left him extremely depressed and he stopped going to classes and just hung out with friends who were only interested in drugs and alcohol. At the end of this first semester an adviser from the school called to tell us that Larry was on the verge of being expelled; they had been unable to contact him for almost two weeks.

This news was so disturbing to me that I took the shuttle from Boston to Washington, D.C., the next morning, rented a car, and drove to his dormitory. One of the boys there told me he sometimes showed up at the cafeteria for lunch just before it closed at 2 p.m. I waited there until 1:45, when a dirty, unshaven, disgusting-looking Larry walked into the cafeteria with two other similar-looking young men. When I confronted Larry, the first thing he did, as only Larry could, was rush up to me and give me a big hug and a kiss and said, "Pop, I am so glad to see you!" After a long talk, I felt more sorry for him than angry, but I told him that I would not stand for his current behavior. He answered that his plan was to leave school and travel to California in his Toyota with his St. Bernard dog named Rosie; the two of them were inseparable. I told him he could do whatever he wished as long as he phoned me at least once a week. I then reached into my wallet and handed him six $100 bills and told him that from that moment on he would have to support himself.

After nine months of traveling Larry ended up in Los Angeles. Then, one day Larry found himself on the street, without a car, his clothes, his wallet, or his dog. He had nothing left in the world, except his underpants, so I suggested he come to live with us in New Hampshire. I told him that I had bought a beautiful piece of property on a lake only a few minutes from the Centronics factory and office. I had selected a builder and architect to build a house for me and had just placed a house trailer on the property for a watchman to live in while taking care of all the construction materials as the house was being built. I told him that he could live in a trailer and do this job while deciding where he wanted to live and what he would do next. He instantly took me up on the offer and said he could also work for the contractor as a carpenter because he had done some carpentry work on his way to California. I told him that would be up to the contractor, not me.

Of course I made all of this up. I had to rush out and buy an old house trailer to put on the property before Larry arrived. And I told the contractor to hire Larry. But what made Larry happiest of all is that a month after he came to New Hampshire, his St. Bernard, Rosie, was found in Los Angeles. My cousin in California arranged to have the dog shipped back east. This was a crowning moment in the life of Larry Howard, the reunion of a man and his dog, which he loved more than anyone or anything in the world.

Down but not out, my son Larry arrives in New Hampshire in 1971.

After several months of hard work, Larry decided to go to summer school to become a veterinarian. With his good grades, I was then able to get him into the pre-med program at the University of New Hampshire, where he decided to be a medical doctor instead. From that point on he was a straight-A student, largely through the positive influence of a young lady named Judy who would eventually become his wife. Later, he was accepted to The New York Medical College, where he switched his interest from orthopedics to psychiatry, and eventually became the chief resident psychiatrist at Long Island Jewish Hospital. But three years later Larry would have another change of mind. He had decided to be a businessman, not a psychiatrist. So he enrolled in the MBA program at New York University. Before long he would join me in forming my next company. But I'm getting ahead of my story again.

THE YEAR 1971 WAS A BUSY ONE. Not only was I building the house in New Hampshire and running Centronics, it was also the year I married Lenore. She had planned to move to New Hampshire about a year after we got married. This would give her the time she needed to wind up her interior design business in New York City and leave her free to be anywhere without obligations other than to her two children who were both in college. Once the house on the lake was built, my personal life was well under control. But Lenore actually ended up spending very little time in New Hampshire, which she found boring since she had no friends there. She preferred staying at our apartment in New York City or at our luxurious duplex penthouse apartment at the Cricket Club in Florida. That was fine by me, as it kept her out of my hair when I needed time for business and two of my children, Larry and Ellen, who were with me in New Hampshire.

During this time Centronics was growing at an incredible pace. We offered our dot matrix printer with the Centronics interface to almost everyone in the world who manufactured small computer systems. Even though we managed to raise our production to 300 printers per day, we still could not satisfy the substantial needs of the market. Everyone who had a personal computer wanted one of these printers since it was the only printer of its type and price then available on the world market.

But a successful product alone does not necessarily make a successful company. There is a big difference between the two, because once you have a product you have to take it to the marketplace. Then you have to develop credibility and acceptance of the product and its reliability. Once that's done, you have to have the ability to mass-produce it. Once you're in the mass production mode, what you do has to be profitable. And you have to have all the bells, whistles, accessories, interfaces, and know-how for all of these things to be able to get broader acceptance of your product to sustain growth.

One way we did this at Centronics was by establishing a sales and service presence and offices in fifty-three different countries worldwide. This came about as a result of a new philosophy that I introduced to the OEM manufacturers who purchased our printers and sold them under their own names as part of their systems. Usually, each company must train its own service people and stock a supply of all parts to quickly repair defective machines. But this represented a very substantial investment and an additional management structure for manufacturers. So Centronics set up a universal service with a stock of spare parts that could provide service for a dozen or more different OEM manufacturers in each of these locations, instead of each company having its own service department for the printers. This innovative approach for an OEM supplier such as Centronics made our products much more desirable. It also made it easy for new manufacturers to change the outdated printers in their product line and introduce new updated systems to their customers worldwide without the usual substantial investment in parts inventory or the training of service people. And since we wanted to remain the dominant OEM supplier to the computer industry, we began offering an entire spectrum of printer types, some slower but cheaper, others faster but more expensive.

NEEDLESS TO SAY, with all this going on—the success of Centronics, the homes to take care of in several cities, my business travel worldwide, and trying to keep my new wife and family together and happy—I was somewhat remiss in my relationship with my daughter, Ellen. She was busy at Boston University, where she also worked for two years in the office of BU's Heart Surgeon for Exercise Physiology. She also took care of her dog and two horses, which she rode and competed with regularly. I would occasionally have dinner with her at Legal Seafood, her favorite fish restaurant in Boston, but I failed to notice that she was getting thinner and thinner. When I learned that her weight was down to 85 from her usual 105 pounds, I spoke to a few knowledgeable medical people and decided that she needed to see a psychiatrist to evaluate her ailment, which I suspected was anorexia.

After months of seeing several psychiatrists, some of whom were more helpful than others, Ellen's weight was down to seventy pounds and she ended up being hospitalized. This was an emotionally draining experience for me, with little support from Lee, Ellen's mother and my ex-wife. But it all came to an abrupt end in a most unexpected fashion when I sought treatment for my own problem, "executive depression."

Though my business affairs were going incredibly well, I felt depressed at times and I couldn't understand why. A friend of mine suggested that I see a German-born psychiatrist in Westport, Connecticut, named Dr. Tec. In the course of my one-on-one meetings with him, I discussed Ellen's anorexia, as the troubles with my daughter were in some measure responsible for my own depression. Dr. Tec said that in his practice he had had a 100 percent success rate using a European medication on a dozen anorexic patients who were emotionally and psychologically ready to be cured. He told me to bring Ellen to his office for an interview to determine if this medication was right for her. After his second visit with Ellen, he said he was confident the medication would work on her.

Within a matter of days you could see the change in Ellen's general attitude and new eating habits. And within a couple of weeks it was obvious that she was well on her way to gaining weight and would no longer be plagued by this illness. Ellen's life returned to normal and she was able to complete her schoolwork and focus on her competitive riding. After one brief unsuccessful marriage to a restaurateur, she met Jim Toon, the owner of JT Farm in South Salem, New York, where Ellen kept her horses. They eventually married and Ellen is a very happy person. She is closer to me today than she has ever been.

On the horse, my daughter, Ellen Toon, at the JT Farm in South Salem, New York

THE WINTER WEEKENDS I spent in Florida while living and working in New Hampshire were a great relaxation. I had bought one of the new, super-luxurious condominiums at the Cricket Club. Cliff Perlman of Caesars Palace had one of the four duplex penthouse apartments and I purchased the one remaining penthouse apartment. Lenore, who was an interior designer, furnished the apartment lavishly and decorated a room on the roof deck of the apartment with items we had brought back from an African safari vacation.

Lenore would spend her winters at our apartment in Florida while I commuted on the weekends. Each Thursday afternoon during the winter months, I would fly down to Miami to enjoy a relaxing weekend of tennis and swimming in Florida's fine weather before returning to Boston early Monday morning. I made many friends in this high-rise building, including Arnold Walliwitz, who was in the real estate business. One day during a discussion with Arnold and a friend of his named Joe Jacobs, who worked in the real estate division of Bear Stearns, the topic came up of an office building for sale on Second Avenue and 43rd Street in New York. A sales contract on the building that had been signed almost two years before was expiring in the following week. The contract called for the purchase price of $10 million to be paid in six days. The owner of the contract was prepared to let it expire but was willing to sell it for only $100,000. That was quite a deal since the $10 million price was 30 percent to 40 percent lower than the current market value of the building.

We all agreed to take over this contract to purchase the building. I would put up the $10.1 million required to make this purchase and would own 70 percent of the building. Once we obtained a mortgage, I would be repaid most of my $10.1 million purchase price and Arnold and Joe would each own 15 percent of the building, after putting up their 15 percent share of the money. They would be responsible for managing it and taking care of the construction needed to upgrade the entrance lobby and the windows of the building.

The corner of the building was rented to a group of investors and a very experienced restaurateur who planned on opening a high-class restaurant called Jake's Steak House. When Jake's was about to open, they decided they needed more space in the basement beyond what they had. We had the space, but they would not accept the additional rent we wanted to charge. After a great deal of haggling, they suggested that Joe, Arnold, and I could eat there free whenever we wanted, as long as we paid the tax and tipped the waiter. We accepted this and enjoyed our meals at Jake's for the next four years until the restaurant went bankrupt.

About five years later we decided to sell the fully rented building. To get the best price, we had to redo the lobby, as originally planned. Arnold, who was a builder on Long Island, took charge of the construction. But after twice the time and more than twice the budget we had planned to do the job, it was still unfinished. The contractors were Arnold's friends and we suspected that there were some deals between them, so we threw them off the job and hired our own contractors to finish so that we could sell the building. Unfortunately, due to the delays, the market for office buildings went soft. A year later we sold the building for $25 million, which was still a nice profit and, other than in its final days, a fun investment.

BY THE MID-1970S, COMPUTERS COULD HANDLE color very easily but there was no satisfactory low-cost color printer available for the emerging personal computer market. To satisfy this untapped market, Centronics developed the first multiple-pass color matrix printer. Just as color typewriters used color ribbons, this matrix printer used three color ribbons. It would take three passes of the printhead to print each line in color. The red, yellow, and blue ribbons, either alone or in combination gave you seven colors, as well as black.

At the same time, we developed the first desktop laser printer. It all came about when I hosted a visit by the head of engineering of Canon, at the request of Fujio Mitarai, who had graduated from MIT and was the son of the chairman of Canon; today he is the chairman. He wanted to send someone to study Centronics and the way we worked, and I insisted that he return the favor for me. Mitarai subsequently gave me a personal tour of the Canon facility, where I saw that they were making a large laser printer, which was the size of a dining room table and cost more than $200,000. Only the largest companies that needed to do a great deal of black-and-white printing could afford such a laser printer. When I saw it, I suggested to Mitarai that maybe we could make a desktop version of laser printer together; it would use semiconductor lasers and be no larger than our original dot matrix printer.

Ahead of its time: the interior of a prototype of the Canon-Centronics Laser Printer (1975)

And that's exactly what we ended up doing—Canon did the copier portion of it and Centronics did the electronics and the printhead. We managed to miniaturize the electronics using a semiconductor laser instead of a big powerful laser. The semiconductor laser, which then cost $10,000 each, is a mass production item today and it costs $7 apiece, despite ten times the inflation. Almost all the desktop laser printers today are based on this invention. But we couldn't complete the project because the technology of the copier at the time was too cumbersome and too large. In the end, I gave up the project and Canon took it over themselves. The desktop laser printer didn't become reality until many years later when Canon developed the removable photosensitive drum that could be easily changed by the user.

By 1975 Centronics had sold more than 40,000 medium-speed printers and introduced a new series of four impact printers, which we called the 500 Series. The line ranged in speed from 100 to 660 characters per second, compared to the 165 to 330 character per second range of the earlier models. Centronics was extremely profitable and the board decided to pay a dividend of 25 cents each quarter. Since I had several million shares, I would receive several million dollars a year as a dividend from Centronics. The personal tax rate for that income was 80 percent, a quite unfair tax on money that a corporation had already paid taxes on. At that time there were so many tax shelter schemes that I felt I needed some professional advice on how best to deal with my enormous tax burden. To manage my financial matters, I hired two young men named Sheldon Claar and Seymour Goldblatt who were managing the very large net worth of Charles Stewart Mott, the grandson of the man who helped shape General Motors, beginning as a parts supplier. With my help, Shel and Sy started their own company called S Squared to manage the holdings of Mott, his sister, and myself.

Both Mott and I were in the same dilemma of needing to shelter a substantial amount of dividend income that was subject to this outrageous tax. We ended up investing a great deal of money in real estate that was usually structured as a limited partnership to have more write-offs than the money you actually invested. In later years the tax laws changed and all of these real estate tax savings were eventually recaptured by the government. Fortunately, under Ronald Reagan, the tax rate was substantially less. When Shel contracted amyotrophic lateral sclerosis (ALS) and died of the disease, Sy with the help of his son continued S Squared Capital II Management, one of the best and largest money management companies in the country. Today Sy is a semiretired multimillionaire.

THE YEAR 1977 ALMOST SAW my involvement in yet another gambling town, Atlantic City. One day, Bill Kauffman, a friend of mine who had gambling casino holdings in Puerto Rico and was in the process of building a hotel casino in Atlantic City, invited me to accompany him there by helicopter to discuss all sorts of electronic control systems, including a casino control system similar to the one we had installed in his casino in Puerto Rico. While there I walked across the street to see a hotel that was under construction. It was to be named the Benihana Hotel and had a Japanese theme. But construction on the hotel was at a standstill because of disputes between the project developer and the individual from Japan who was financing the project.

It just so happens that the Japanese gentleman in charge of the project who was standing there talking with a group of people in the front of the steel structure was someone with whom I had had some dealings in Japan. He was the head of a Japanese conglomerate that wanted to get into the computer printer business and I had advised him on how to position his products in the growing computer printer industry. After some friendly moments of conversation, he explained that because of substantial delays and huge cost overruns he was under great pressure from his board of directors to abandon the project.

I immediately called Don Seigeloub, who was one of my wintertime friends at the Cricket Club in Florida and a builder/developer living in Westport, Connecticut, and told him to get into his car and come to Atlantic City so that we could turn this catastrophe into a winning opportunity. Don and I then spent almost two weeks preparing a very detailed plan that would help salvage the very substantial investment the Japanese man had made in the hotel to date. Unfortunately, the board of directors of the company decided that they did not want to put any more money into this disaster, and my Atlantic City adventure came to an end.

That year I ended up selling Gamex Industries, Inc., with its casino computer system and electronic slot machines, to a company headed by the founder of Bally Manufacturing Co., which was the largest manufacturer of mechanical slot machines. They saw the advantages of an electronic slot machine and its future, and purchased Gamex to acquire its intellectual property and know-how. Today there are tens of thousands of electronic slot machines in casinos all over the world, but my Gamex electronic slot machine was the first.

··19··

Ronald Reagan and Other Disappointments

As Centronics flourished in New Hampshire, we probably became one of the largest employers in the state and with that came a certain political leverage. After taking charge of the 1972 election campaign of Governor Meldrim Thompson, I became something of a political heavyweight. One of my best friends in New Hampshire at the time was William Loeb, the owner and publisher of the *Manchester Union Leader*, which is by far the largest and most influential newspaper in the state. When Ronald Reagan was running to be the Republican Party's nominee for president in 1980, he wanted Bill's support and came to visit him at his home. Bill insisted that I join him for his meeting with Ronald and Nancy Reagan. (We would also have a similar meeting with George H. W. Bush, who was also running for the Republican nomination, accompanied by his young son George.) We sat and talked about almost every subject that Bill and I could think of, including Reagan's congressional agenda, his age, his conservative views, and his experience as the governor of California. This meeting lasted for more than two hours and we all got to know each other quite well. Bill and I agreed to support Ronald Reagan for president.

My support of Ronald Reagan's bid for the presidency in 1980 provided this photo-op for me and my daughter, Ellen Toon.

Winning New Hampshire is often essential to winning the Republican Party's nomination, and obtaining the support of Bill Loeb and the *Manchester Union Leader* is often crucial to winning the New Hampshire primary. While Bill's support came principally through his newspaper, his wife, Nackey, a paraplegic who was confined to a wheelchair, was also extremely active in supporting Ronald Reagan both before and after he received the nomination. My activities were principally fund-raising in the New England area, and being on the Reagan National

Election Committee. Bill Casey, a sometime Road Runner and a friend of mine from Roslyn, had become Reagan's national campaign manager, and I allowed Max Hugel, who at that time was the executive vice-president of Centronics, to work full-time as Casey's assistant in managing Reagan's campaign. As we all know, Ronald Reagan became one of history's finest and most productive presidents.

Bill Loeb, Bill Casey, Max Hugel, and I contributed materially to the election of Ronald Reagan, but in the end he let us down. In 1980, Bill Loeb was diagnosed with an inoperable cancer, and his health was fading fast. I decided to host a dinner in his honor and sent out invitations to about a thousand people whose lives he had touched. I sent a letter to President Reagan months in advance of the dinner asking him to be the principal speaker at this dinner. Having received no word, I tried several times to reach him by phone, and the best I could do was talk to his secretary, whom I knew. She finally told me that he could not attend because of a conflict in his schedule. I then asked if he could send a videotaped message to be shown at the dinner as a small token of his appreciation for all that Bill had done to get him elected president. After all, Ronald Reagan might not have become president if not for Bill Loeb. When I did not get any response to this request, I suggested that President Reagan give Bill a quick call during the dinner when the speeches were being made and say a few kind words to Bill. I never received a reply to this last suggestion and lost all respect for Ronald Reagan as a person. This upset and angered me so much that I never again engaged in any further political activities.

GOOD THINGS SOMETIMES come to an abrupt ending, and Centronics was no exception. In the late 1970s, we began to notice numerous random firing of the solenoids causing some failures in our newest printer and the first to be built completely in-house, the Mini Printer Model 770. All seven of the solenoids would begin to fire continuously like a machine gun, the power supply would start to smoke and burn, and the printer would turn off. This defect in the microprocessor of the printer was occurring randomly and without warning on our recently produced machines. Because this posed a fire hazard, we had no choice but to recall and refund the money to everyone who had purchased one of these machines, which had been manufactured in the previous four months. That event marked the abrupt end to the prosperous years at Centronics.

Upon investigation we found that the problem was caused by the microprocessor that controls all the functions in the printer. The vendor for this essential part was a small company that we had selected during the initial testing of the printer because they were able to very quickly react to our requirements for engineering changes to the chip. This enabled us to bring this revolutionary product to the market very quickly. But now, facing the pressures of huge demand, they had implemented, without our authorization, a change to the chip that increased their yield so that they could satisfy our production demands. But the device had not been tested.

Under normal conditions, most companies would be forced into bankruptcy when such a catastrophic event occurred. But fortunately Centronics had $196 million in cash or its equivalent in Puerto Rican bonds. We had located a factory in Puerto Rico a number of years earlier and had totally automated the production of the main printed circuit board, which was extremely profitable because its sales price was based on having it hand-produced in New Hampshire. We had opened this factory because of a unique tax law in Puerto Rico that exempted U.S.-based companies from federal tax laws. When this law was passed, Puerto Rico was principally an agricultural country and the tax exemption was put into effect to attract labor-intensive industrial businesses like Centronics to locate manufacturing facilities in their country. As a result we had in Puerto Rico substantial profits that we invested in Puerto Rican tax-exempt bonds. The $196 million allowed Centronics to honor its obligation to have the thousands of printers that were sold with this defective chip returned to us for a full refund, and still remain financially solvent.

At this point running Centronics was more of a chore than a joy. But before moving on, I felt it was my duty to get the company back to being an industry leader again, particularly since Japanese manufacturers had quickly copied our designs and were now manufacturing similar products. The big question was: How could I preserve the equity in the substantial stock positions that my family, my friends, and I held in the company, and how could I get out?

I needed a plan. After a great deal of thought and discussions with other people whose opinions I respect, a friend of mine on Wall Street named Wilbur Ross came up with a company that might solve my problem as well as that company's problem all at once. That company was Control Data Corp. They had a printer division called Computer Peripherals Inc., and that division manufactured all the printers needed by Control Data, National Cash Register, and International Computer Ltd. Now that numerous companies were producing printers that were being connected to mini computers and small personal computers via the Centronics interface, Control Data's printer division could no longer produce printers for these three companies that were competitive in price or technology. As a result, Control Data was trying to dispose of its printer division.

Wilbur Ross and I came up with a proposal whereby Control Data's printer division would be merged into Centronics, their printer division management would assume the management of the new, expanded Centronics, and Control Data would invest $100 million in a cash purchase of Centronics shares and take over control of the board of Centronics. This plan was implemented except, during negotiations, the dollar amount of the stock purchase was reduced to $54 million. My associates and I would resign from the company and the board of directors so that Control Data could appoint their own board of directors and have complete control of the company, as a subsidiary. Control Data offered to buy all of my shares at $14 a share, which was the price at that time. But I felt the company was worth a great deal more, especially since we were starting substantial deliveries on our recently signed IBM contract for our new dot matrix printer for business applications, which had a nine-pin head instead of seven and provided 30 percent higher-quality printing than the original Model 101.

I simply resigned as the chairman, but for appearance purposes remained as a member of the board of the company, but only for a few months. Being on the board was an agonizing experience because I saw that the board was taking actions that were in the best interests of Control Data rather than Centronics, which was still an independent public company listed on the New York Stock Exchange. A year and a half after my resignation, I notified all of my friends and relatives in advance of my intentions to sell my personal shares. In about one month, I sold all of my shares at an average price of $21.

In keeping with my plan, I had an idea for a new technology that could be used as part of a small color printer system. Before I resigned from the board I offered this idea to the new Centronics board of directors, but they rejected this proposed project because they did not want to make the substantial investment that would be required to develop this technology into a product. I documented this rejection and received the necessary release of any claims regarding this new idea. Two years later I would form a new company called Howtek, Inc., to carry out this mission.

··20··

From Printers to Scanners

WITH MY DEPARTURE FROM CENTRONICS late in 1982, I decided to sell my house on the lake in New Hampshire, which had been my primary residence for a dozen years, and move back to New York City. The buyer was Max Hugel, who after being the deputy director of the CIA when Bill Casey was CIA director decided to live in New Hampshire since he had a number of business and other investments that he had made in the state during his tenure as a vice-president with Centronics.

Lenore and I bought a 10,000-square-foot apartment on 72nd Street. In addition to the $2.2 million purchase price we also invested about $1 million to completely renovate this magnificent but old-fashioned prewar apartment, which had a 52-foot-long living room with a fireplace so large that you could walk into it, as well as seven small maid's rooms. I very much enjoyed designing and rebuilding this apartment in such a way as to incorporate my office into the apartment.

Shortly after moving to New York City, while working in my personal laboratory on my next invention, I did something on a lark. Two of my friends, Bob Mittman and Billy Walters, had a personal interest in a police organization called the Westchester County Society for the Prevention of Cruelty to Children (SPCC). In order to be on the board of directors of this very worthwhile organization, candidates had to enroll in the police-training program at John Jay College. This sounded like fun so I signed up with them, and we each ended up with an associate's degree in criminal justice. We also had to pass a shooting test at the police department's firing range, so that we would be qualified to carry a gun.

In order to retain this permit to carry a concealed weapon, there are specific minimum requirements for a police officer's level of activity. One requirement is being involved in the collar, arrest, and prosecution of at least one criminal each year. Our first opportunity occurred one night when I received a phone call at about 11 p.m. from Kenny Ellman, who was director of the SPCC, instructing me to come immediately to Westchester County police headquarters, together with Bob and Billy. When we arrived, Kenny told us about drug dealings with children at a local high school. One of the boys that Kenny used as a source at that school gave Kenny the address of a place he had been told to go to pick up a supply of drugs for himself and others at the school. Kenny, two other SPCC officers, and the three of us were scheduled to raid this drug distribution apartment in the Harlem section of upper Manhattan. Bob, Billy, and I had our guns and were raring to go.

When we arrived at the building, Kenny assigned to the three of us the task of protecting the perimeter of the building in case anyone tried to escape out the front or rear doors or used one of the fire escapes. I don't know about Bob and Billy, but I was really scared. After a very long half hour, Kenny and his two associates came out the front door with a giant, 350-pound, muscular, six-foot-three individual, his arms hand-cuffed behind him and his ankles handcuffed, so as to only permit small steps. They loaded him into their police car and told us to follow them back to the police station. We had to be there to attest to the fact that we were part of the collar and sign the police arrest report.

We all walked up two flights of a narrow wooden staircase to the SPCC's small office together with this huge prisoner in order to fill out all the necessary paperwork. Kenny released one handcuff from the wrists of the prisoner and attached it to a two-inch-diameter pipe of a large cast-iron radiator. After about an hour of paperwork the prisoner said he had to go to the bathroom, and we all passed the buck as to who should take him. After about ten minutes of bickering, he began shouting at us, then put both arms around the radiator and lifted it, breaking it away from the wall and releasing the handcuff that was on the pipe. At that point Kenny escorted him to the bathroom himself without further incident.

At about 3:30 a.m. we were free to leave, having had a most exciting and memorable evening and feeling happy that we had survived. Since 1982 I have been on the board of directors of the SPCC with the title of deputy commissioner. In that capacity I have attended the regularly scheduled board meetings and made substantial personal and financial contributions to the organization, as the funding that it receives from the state is insufficient to sustain its very worthwhile operations. As a token of their appreciation for my loyal uncompensated contribution for more than twenty-five years as a deputy commissioner, I've been presented a beautiful plaque, designating my appointment to the "Police Hall of Fame."

IN THE MEANTIME, with no conscious intent to earn a future appointment to the Printer Hall of Fame, I personally began developing a low-cost color printer for the fast-growing personal computer market. I wanted to be able to print in color on plain paper. I spent about two years doing hundreds of experiments and spent several million dollars but I finally managed to develop the revolutionary technology that would lead to the Pixelmaster printer.

The invention that led to this printer was twofold. First, I decided to use "hot melt" ink, a solid ink that when heated becomes liquid. If the printing dot produced with that liquid was small enough, it would solidify immediately. The mechanism I chose to spit out the ink was a piezo crystal, which had never been used in a printer before. A piezo crystal can generate an electric potential in response to applied mechanical stress. The best-known device using a piezo crystal is the electric cigarette lighter; pressing the button causes a spring-loaded hammer to hit a piezoelectric crystal, producing a sufficiently high voltage that an electric current flows across a small spark gap, thus heating and igniting the gas.

I worked on using a piezo crystal for printing until I found a method and configuration that would enable the crystals to fire millions of small droplets of ink of each of the primary colors — red, green, and blue — as well as black, onto a piece of paper. Every dot had to hit a precise location and it had to happen quickly enough to produce a color page in less than two minutes. It was a monumental task, but I succeeded. Almost every color ink-jet printer today — and there are millions — uses piezoelectric crystals to control the flow of ink from the printhead to the paper.

Once I had decided that this technology could, in fact, work, the next step was to actually design a product around this new technology. That was the beginning of a company I called Howtek, my twenty-sixth, to which I contributed this intellectual property without compensation, as well as $4 million in working capital in exchange for most of the stock in the company as my founder's stock. For months I had been on the lookout for engineering executives who could make a complete and cohesive management team. I identified six individuals from various companies who were currently employed and as a group would fit the bill to form a well-rounded starting organization, and I went out and hired them.

I then called upon the prime connections and affiliations I had established in Japan while at Centronics. I contacted a company called Juki, which was similar in some ways to Brother. Juki's main business was manufacturing the finest industrial sewing machines in the world. Since I had a marvelous reputation in Japan for creating a new industry around the very successful Centronics dot matrix printer, Juki was quick to recognize that my presentation offered them a unique business opportunity. They were eager to participate in the development of the Pixelmaster. Juki proved to be a marvelous partner; they were completely dedicated to this project. Together we produced about a hundred Pixelmaster color printers that were to be used for beta testing and customer samples to start the sales process. After making some minor changes along the way, the end result was an outstanding color printer.

NOT LONG AFTER HOWTEK'S FOUNDING, however, the company almost lost its chief innovator and funder—me. The story begins with CJ, who was my driver, houseman, and bodyguard. When Lenore and I had moved into the new apartment, CJ had moved in with us. He had been totally devoted to taking care of everything for me, twenty-four hours a day, seven days a week for the previous five years. He had no family of his own and as a result became part of my family. When I needed to travel, he would leave the night before I did, take my luggage, rent a car, set up my clothes in the hotel room, and come to the airport to pick me up upon arrival. It's hard to describe what a warm and wonderful man he was and how close our relationship was.

In our new apartment, CJ lived in separate quarters that we had prepared for him and our housekeeper and cook. To my great surprise, he ended up having an affair with her. It seemed like CJ's only other interest was betting on the horses. One day he mentioned wanting to attend the upcoming Belmont Stakes race in Queens, New York, but on the day of this race, he offered to drive me to the Hamptons and not go to the track. I insisted that he go, so he left early in the morning to make a day of it, which was one of the very few days he ever took off.

On that beautiful, warm summer day in 1985 Lenore and I decided to visit some friends who owned a house in East Hampton. On the way we stopped off to play some tennis and have lunch at the Fresh Meadow Country Club. We then started to drive to the Hamptons in my Rolls-Royce, which CJ usually drove. We were both rather tired as the car sped along the Long Island Expressway. Unfortunately, Lenore took a nap and I had the car on the automatic speed control set at sixty-five miles an hour and was listening to some soft music. The combination of being tired and having had a big lunch caused me to fall asleep at the wheel. The car gradually drifted off to the right-hand shoulder and smashed into the aluminum guardrails. Fortunately, because I was driving a Rolls-Royce, the car tore through about 75 feet of guardrails as though it were an Army tank and ended up hanging partially over an overpass.

The next thing I remember was the rescue people helping my wife out of her side of the car. She had only superficial injuries. I was bleeding profusely from the face and head, and was taken by ambulance to a nearby hospital where they were able to reduce the bleeding, reset my broken nose and dislocated shoulder, and tape my chest to secure the three fractured ribs. It took 165 stitches to piece the skin on my head and face back together. Fortunately my wife had telephoned my brother-in-law, Murray Fuhrman, who arrived at the hospital before any stitches were attempted. He immediately insisted that a plastic surgeon, rather than a young emergency room doctor, do the stitches. I was in the hospital about ten days and then required a hospital bed in my new 72nd Street apartment to continue my recovery.

I found it strange that during my ten days in the hospital, CJ never once came to visit me. But the evening of the day that I returned to my New York apartment, he walked in to my bedroom with tears in his eyes, saying, "Boss, I let you down, and because I let you down you had this accident that was completely my fault." Without giving me the opportunity to console him, he walked out of the room, and with his possessions already packed in a suitcase, he left the apartment without telling anyone where he was going.

For the next two years I did all I could to try to find CJ, but to no avail. Finally, one of my employees told me that while visiting Las Vegas he had seen CJ working in a video store as either a clerk or a manager. As quickly as I could I went to Las Vegas to see him, going directly to the video store from the airport. It was important to me to see that he was physically and emotionally healthy, as he had always been much more than an employee to me. I also wanted to pay him the salary that was his due and give him a departure bonus as a little token of my appreciation for all his years of dedicated service. He hugged and kissed me when he saw me and was extremely happy to hear that I had no lingering injuries from that accident.

We went out for dinner that evening and had a pleasant time reliving some of the memorable moments that we had together. I was able to convince him to accept an envelope from me, which contained his unpaid salary and severance bonus as well as some stock in my new company, Howtek. The next morning I returned to work in New York. I did tell our housekeeper about seeing him in Las Vegas and gave her his phone number. She quickly contacted him because she too had not heard a word from him in two years. About two weeks later she quit her job with us and moved to Las Vegas to marry him. They lived happily in Las Vegas for several years until CJ died of cancer. I am left with many very fond memories of my friend. In his will, he left me a pocket watch that his father had given him when he graduated college. This watch is now part of my watch collection.

HOWTEK AND JUKI SPENT TENS OF MILLIONS of dollars developing the Pixelmaster, which drew interest from various quarters. Apple Computer, which had been a customer of our dot matrix printers, was very interested in the Pixelmaster based on their testing and its estimated pricing. Apple had a desperate need for an affordable color printer and the Pixelmaster was by far the best solution available at that time. During the first six months of testing prior to the start of delivery, Apple forecast a need for 3,000 Pixelmasters per month based on the results we had achieved.

Meanwhile, a man by the name of John Evans, a highly placed executive in Rupert Murdoch's News Corp., was searching for a way to electronically transmit and print a newspaper in color directly in a customer's home. He was enamored by the Pixelmaster demonstration he had seen and quickly arranged for me to meet with Rupert Murdoch in the News Corp. offices in New York. After several hours of discussion with Murdoch and an examination of a financial report furnished by his investment banking firm, Murdoch stated that he wanted to buy Howtek and use the Pixelmaster as a vehicle to print his newspapers in people's homes. Since Howtek had sufficient working capital, I only allowed him to buy 25 percent of the company, mostly from existing employee shareholders and about 5 percent from me. Not selling the entire company was a stupid decision on my part; he would have paid a good deal more than the company was worth. Years later News Corp. would have to sell all of its holdings in Howtek and other companies that it invested in, in order to satisfy pressure from its banks.

Early on Howtek ran into a serious problem, however. A competitor by the name of Data Products conducted a patent infringement litigation against us for a patent that they had recently purchased from another company involving the use of hot melt ink. We fought the infringement claim and we were about to receive a favorable decision from the judge in New Hampshire, when Data Products, realizing they were going to lose this case, decided to withdraw their suit.

In the course of due diligence on this suit, however, Data Products learned that we used different shapes for each color ink, so that a user couldn't put the wrong ink into the wrong slot. Almost two years later Data Products was issued a patent based on the way the solid ink pieces were color coded with different shapes. That patent would never hold up in patent court because we had prior art, meaning that a patent on that invention would not be valid. They had simply stolen it from us. But that was irrelevant, because they presented their patent to the International Trade Commission, which does not rule on the validity of any patent and simply accepts an issued patent as a valid one. If an imported device appears to infringe

Stuck in port: The much anticipated Pixelmaster, a low-cost color printer for the fast-growing personal computer market, on exhibit, with me and a product engineer from Juki, the printer's manufacturer

that patent, the device is held in a port of entry until such time as the case is won or lost. These cases usually take years and millions of dollars to litigate. A two-year delay and a substantial cost for us is exactly what Data Products accomplished by sponsoring this litigation.

During those two years, the value of the yen rose from 245 to the dollar to 125 to the dollar. As a result the Pixelmaster that Juki was manufacturing for us cost us almost twice as much as it did two years earlier, because our contract price was in yen, not dollars. The Pixelmaster now became what I called a "tweener," as it was too costly for its intended market, owners of personal computers, and not of a quality high enough (dots per inch) to produce the color pages required for a proof by the graphic arts industry. Although the litigation ended up as a victory in the courts for Howtek, by depriving the company of products or customers for two years, it ended up being terribly destructive. Howtek now had to fight for its life.

LIKE MANY OF MY FRIENDS, Bert Miller, with whom I played tennis two or three times a week for years, had invested a substantial amount of money in Howtek shares. But with the company reporting losses every quarter for a couple of years, he sustained a substantial loss. So Miller decided to sell his Howtek stock and take a loss on it to save paying some of the taxes he had due on his real estate profits, but he could not repurchase these shares for at least six months. Almost a year later, seeing that the price of Howtek stock was at about the same low point for some time, he thought that it might be the right time to reinstate his stock position in Howtek.

Of course, whenever anyone asked me, "How is the company doing?" I would always respond, "We're doing fine," or "You know that I can't answer that question." Unfortunately, the day after we played tennis, he called his broker and bought a number of shares equal to what he had originally owned in one large transaction. The manner in which his young broker handled the purchase of these Howtek shares gave the appearance that he was reacting to some inside information. I did not admit or deny any wrongdoing, which is the standard practice in handling matters like this. Even though I was in no way financially involved in this transaction, the SEC imposed a civil penalty of $40,000 on me. I also had to agree that I would never do any such a thing ever again. Of course, I never would and never have.

SINCE ITS START IN 1984, and in the two dozen years that followed, Howtek was in five different businesses, introduced four unsuccessful products, was run by three unsuccessful CEOs, and should have gone bankrupt at least three times, but I always gave it the financial support it needed to continue, including $16 million after the Pixelmaster debacle. Eventually Howtek eased itself out of the printer business and began to develop, manufacture, and market digitizing systems, which are now commonly known as scanners.

In 1987 Howtek began development of its first scanner with the goal of delivering a smaller, easier to use, and less costly alternative to traditional scanners on the market at that time. Sharp had introduced a color copier that contained a desktop-size digital scanner with a color copier in a single package. This digital product could not compete with the existing analog color copiers. So I convinced Sharp to just sell me the desktop color scanner portion of the machine.

This "failed product" became the new, very inexpensive Howtek Color Scanner. Howtek followed with a series of products further improving the quality of digital imaging while reducing the price and complexity of digitizing systems. The scanners converted printed, photographic, and other hard copy images to digital form for use in the graphic arts, photo finishing, and medical industries.

But Howtek's only successful product ended up being a desktop color scanner designed for use by the medical equipment industry to scan and digitalize X-rays. This success would lead to Howtek's eventual transformation into a medical imaging company.

··21··

Love Life

I LED A VERY ACTIVE CREATIVE LIFE. I also led a very active love life. The two were closely intertwined. Put simply, I had a lust for new and different things, be they inventions, businesses—or women.

By the early 1980s, Lenore and I were in the twilight years of our marriage, arguing about insignificant things all the time. Since I had bought the apartment on East 72nd Street as part of my real estate investment portfolio, I decided to sell the apartment and move to a new condominium project in Manhasset, Long Island. Lenore wanted to live in that area because she had many friends there who all belonged to the same country club. We sold our apartment on the Upper East Side of Manhattan to the entertainer Billy Joel, and Lenore quickly and very nicely furnished our condominium, which had a clubhouse and six clay tennis courts.

Lenore and I were officially separated by 1983. In the settlement, aside from the cash and bonds, Lenore kept the condominium in Manhasset. I had an apartment at the Excelsior on 57th Street that I kept, which I had been using as my office. Though the divorce would take some time to complete, as Lenore kept adding to her demands, I was a single man again, free to do what I wanted, when I wanted to do it.

I pledged that I would never marry again since I was already sixty years old.

But my attraction to beautiful women went undiminished. Shortly after my separation from Lenore, I attended an art showing in lower Manhattan where I was introduced to a gorgeous, twenty-two-year-old French-German girl by the name of Hannah. She was looking for a rich boyfriend and I fit the bill perfectly. She quickly moved into my 57th Street apartment, which she liked having to herself whenever I was away, which was often.

One day my friend Norman Braman, a successful owner of several car dealerships in Miami and South Florida whom I had known since 1955, invited us to his daughter's wedding at the Plaza Hotel in New York. My ex-wife Lenore had also been invited to the wedding, as she had long been friends with Norman and his wife, Irma, as well. Since the wedding promised to be quite an extravaganza, I went out and bought Hannah a beautiful gown and borrowed a very expensive diamond necklace from a friend who was a jeweler on 47th Street and my mentor when it came to buying antique pocket watches. I wore my Armani tuxedo and together Hannah and I looked like we should be on the cover of *Vogue*.

Shortly after we arrived at the wedding, Lenore came into the room and spotted us chatting and having a drink, not far from the elevated entrance stairs. After staring at me with Hannah on my arm for a few minutes she simply turned around and left without ever seeing or saying hello to Norman, Irma, or the bride-to-be.

After a few months Hannah ended up spending most of her time in my penthouse apartment at the Cricket Club in North Miami Beach, as I thought it best not to expose the children to my relationship with her. That left me free to take care of my business in New Hampshire and my children in New York and New Hampshire. This suited Hannah quite well, as she loved being in Florida, and would only have to entertain me for a few days each month when I came down to Florida. She spent most of her time in the roof room doing oil paintings and working as a sales person at a local art gallery owned by a mutual friend.

It was a hectic time for me, but I was living the kind of life as a single man that no one could ever match. I had everything under control with three homes and women everywhere at my beck and call. With Hannah in Florida, I filled the gap in my social life when I was in New York by dating Sandy Sorrento. She was a lot of fun and looking for a rich husband. Even though our relationship was quite serious, I was not prepared to consider getting married again, and that eventually put an end to the relationship.

In 1985, as Lenore was taking our divorce into overtime, I passed up a chance to be a minority owner of a football team. Norman Braman, whose daughter's wedding I had attended a few years earlier, bought the Philadelphia Eagles football team for $68 million that year. I had helped him obtain financing on $60 million, leaving only $8 million remaining to invest. Norm offered his brother-in-law Ed Lefkowitz and me 25 percent each to participate as co-owners. I told Norman that although I would like to go to all the games as if I were an owner, I did not want to be a minority owner. As a result, Ed took 35 percent instead of 25 percent, but sold it back to Norm after one year, for the same reasons that I chose not to be Norm's partner in the first place. During the next ten years Norm and I had great times together in Miami, at the football games, and later in France. Ten years later the Eagles would be sold for $198 million. That huge profit gave Norm an even bigger head than he had before he owned the team.

In 1985, Kit Smith came into my life. I had spent the morning that we first met in a meeting with Lenore for the signing of the final financial settlement in our divorce, which she had previously agreed to. Unfortunately, now for the third time, she insisted on receiving additional compensation over and above the very substantial settlement in the agreement we were to sign that day. I very angrily said that I would not give her another dime, and if she did not sign this agreement, then I would just as soon go to court and let a judge decide what was fair compensation for being married to me for eleven years.

I then walked out and drove my car to the 21 Club, where I was meeting my friend Billy Walters, who had asked me to join him for lunch. We were not due to meet for another hour, but I was so upset over the aborted signing of my settlement agreement with Lenore that I decided to just sit in the car, push the seat back, and listen to some music until it was time to have lunch with Billy. He had said he had an important person to introduce me to at this lunch meeting.

At the appropriate time I walked into the restaurant and saw him sitting at a table with a very attractive woman. When I walked up to the table, Billy Walters introduced me to Kit, and I sat down and ordered a screwdriver. Though I was still very upset over my run-in with Lenore that morning, I found Kit's sense of humor in the course of the lunch quite refreshing. When we finished, I asked Kit for her phone number and wrote it down in my notebook, which I always carried in my back pocket. The number she gave me was the number of the firm where she was employed as a broker. I must have called a dozen times or more over the next three months, but she was never in and she never responded to the numerous messages I left for her.

Then out of the blue one day I received a phone call at my office from Kit. She didn't say why she hadn't called, and rather than get into a long story about my dozen phone calls to her, I said that I would very much like to get together with her.

The next Saturday evening, I drove to her apartment on the East Side of Manhattan to pick her up promptly at 7 p.m. I waited in the car, and in about fifteen minutes she came down wearing a very attractive dress that really showed off her figure; I later learned that she is always about fifteen minutes late for appointments. We went to a small French restaurant that she recommended, which I felt was quite upscale and expensive. After a glass or two of fine red wine and a small salad, she ordered a very expensive fish dish; she only took one small bite and left the rest. Although I found her attractive and interesting, as well as pleasant company, I was annoyed that she didn't eat what she had ordered.

It might appear that I was overreacting; it was, after all, such a minor thing. But until I met Kit, I lived a rather frugal life considering the level of my wealth and income. Kit would teach me how to live life high on the hog. Her efforts elevated my standard of living, which I have now enjoyed for more than twenty years. Although her spending has sometimes bothered me, I've come to accept it mainly because I can afford it. Sometimes I jokingly say, "Kit has made a millionaire out of me, but before I met her I was a billionaire."

That was just the beginning of Kit's makeover of Bob Howard. On our second date I took Kit to a private club for dinner and dancing. We were dancing to an old slow song, when she put her hand around my neck and started to feel my hair. I quickly said to her, "If my toupee moves, don't be scared." She stopped dancing, stepped back, and said, rather loudly: "You're wearing a toupee? Take it off!" I did as ordered and put it over the top of a wine bottle on our table. I have never worn a toupee since that day.

From 1985, when I first met Kit, until November 1987, when we were married, we had a whirlwind courtship. While those years were exciting, interesting, and joyful, there were short periods when we didn't see each other and once we even broke up. Oddly enough, the next night we both had dates and accidentally met at the same popular Broadway show, a situation that embarrassed both of us. Later that week, we were together again, and as our relationship became increasingly serious, I met Kit's two children: Jodi was seventeen years old at the time and a senior at a private school in Manhattan, and Brett was fifteen and attending a private school in New Hampshire. The death of their father the previous year had hit both kids very hard. I told them that I would never try to replace their father but just wanted to extend my love and friendship to them.

Life was wonderful with Kit, but marriage was always a subject of our conversations. After about a year and a half, she gave me the ultimatum: if we didn't get married, she was going to leave me. I didn't want that ever to happen, so I agreed.

Although she wanted a short engagement period, I insisted on an extended one. As an excuse, I said that I wanted to get married in our new apartment, which was being rebuilt in the Excelsior. We had been living together in rather crowded conditions with her two children in her East End Avenue apartment. Although she didn't want to live at the Excelsior, I insisted, since I already had my office in the building. We bought the largest apartment in the Excelsior, with magnificent views and plenty of room, but it needed to be gutted and rebuilt, and that would take eight months.

The construction was completed on schedule and all the

new furnishings arrived in time for us to enjoy a small wedding in our new apartment. It was attended by our children, close family members, and a small group of friends, among them Norm Braman, the only man not wearing a tuxedo. Just before the wedding, Western Union delivered a telegram to the apartment addressed to Kit Smith. It said: "Kit, before you marry Bob Howard, having been married to him for eleven years, I would like to give you some advice. If you go ahead with this marriage, you will be making the biggest mistake of your life. I gave him the best eleven years of my life and then he dumped me. After all that, all that I ended up with was a meager $27 million. I hope that you do not fall into the same trap." It was signed Lenore Howard.

Third time lucky: Kit and I in our wedding photo, 1987

Kit was taken in by this telegram and went around showing it to everyone, until she came to Norm Braman, when she realized that it might have been a joke, and she laughingly said to Norm, "You must have sent this." He vehemently denied it. After about ten minutes, I finally admitted that I had sent the telegram. But Lenore didn't get 27 million; she only got 24 million.

Norman had a beautiful home overlooking the Mediterranean in Cap d'Ail, France, where he spent his summers, and I had an open invitation to spend a few days there with him anytime. After our marriage, Kit accompanied me on some business in Germany, and afterward we spent a long weekend together at Norman's house. We found the area so enjoyable and desirable that we began considering the purchase of a second home in Europe. But rather than rushing into a decision, we decided to rent a house the following summer. By that time I had a great deal of business in Germany, which allowed Kit and I to have an incredibly fun summer in a rental house in Cap Ferrat on the Mediterranean within walking distance of a beautiful tennis club with red clay courts. In September of that year I had to go to Japan for a few days and Kit stayed at the rented villa awaiting my return.

Being away made me realize just how much I enjoyed being in France, so I telephoned Kit from Japan and told her to start looking for a permanent home there. When I returned two days later, the real estate agent took us to two old dilapidated monstrosities before showing us a third residence named Villa L'Horizon, which had been totally renovated two years earlier and was furnished with exquisite antiques throughout. When Kit saw it, she said, "If you buy this house, I will never leave you." Knowing this, the next morning I offered the owner what he was asking for the property. We also bought the contents of the villa, which were beautiful and of the highest quality. Six months later we owned and had moved into the Villa L'Horizon.

Not only had Norman been instrumental in getting us to buy the villa in France, but we continued to share business interests as well. In 1984, Norman had become the exclusive master distributor for the Sterling Motorcar Company in the United States. The Sterling was a car made in London by Austin Rover, and Austin Rover was Norman's 50 percent partner. After about four years of building a dealer organization, he needed a good deal of additional financing, and he came to me for help. Since I had some experience in public financing, I arranged all of the necessary underwriting and negotiated a high evaluation for this IPO. Then, with the help of a securities attorney named Irwin Rosenthal, whom I had worked with for years and recommended, Norman wrote the prospectus, and off they went to London together to get the signatures of his partner, Austin Rover, for submission of the prospectus to the Securities and Exchange Commission.

But Austin Rover was appalled at the thought that their U.S. partner wanted to do an IPO, which would make them a publicly owned company, subject to SEC disclosures and regulations. Instead they offered to buy out Norman and his 135 dealers in 1989. In the prospectus, Irwin Rosenthal and I had placed a very high value on the company to reduce the number of shares sold to the public, which was a common practice at that time and kept IPO dilution to a minimum. The end result was that Norman sold his 50 percent share of the company for substantially more than it was actually worth. I was disappointed that Norman never even bothered to thank me for my help in this transaction.

But we were so happy with our home in France that all was forgiven. Our villa overlooked the Mediterranean, and since it was built on the topside of a cliff, we had a clear view of Nice, its beach, and airport from every room in the villa. Our additions to the property included a pool with a movable cover to enable me to swim all year round, a spa that replicated our favorite place in Baden-Baden, Germany, and a funicular to easily get from the main house up to the pool and spa. With the help of a gardener, Kit completely redid the gardens and bought the flowers for planting in the different seasons. After a few years we redid the kitchen because Kit loved cooking and we hired a couple, Roger and Delia, to prepare meals for us. They had an apartment on the property and took good care of us all the years we lived there.

Our kids visited as often as possible. They all loved the villa and the atmosphere of the south of France. Looking back now

A view of the Mediterranean and the city of Nice from the Howard family villa in Cap Ferrat, France.

I think Kit and I miss the food most of all, especially the local outdoor markets where we would get fresh fruits and vegetables every morning. The croissants and palmiers were scrumptious, and the great wines we drank from Bordeaux, Burgundy, Tuscany, and Provence were truly bottles made in heaven.

For the next fifteen years, Villa L'Horizon was our family home.

··22··

A Lust for Color

MEANWHILE, I HAD STARTED my twenty-seventh company.

One day, during a board of directors meeting at Howtek, we discussed an idea I had for a radically different printing concept that would make offset color printing as fast and affordable as black and-white printing. The problem at that time was that offset color was a slow, costly process. It took at least ten days to two weeks of what was called "prepress" preparation before a color print job could even be put on a printing press, and because of this expense it was both impractical and costly to print less than 10,000 copies of anything. I wanted to apply our knowledge of computers and imaging to the color printing business.

With the advances in computer technology, I thought it should be possible to image the printing plates directly on the printing press itself. We had conducted some experiments using the Pixelmaster to put digital information on a rigid paper printing plate that was used by the low-end printing shops. A friend in New Hampshire by the name of Frank Romano, who had a small printing press, was nice enough to run some tests on the printing plates for us so that we could get his expert opinions. He told us that the plates produced by the Pixelmaster had insufficient resolution (not enough dots per inch) for a printing plate, but the idea did work. Although it was an outstanding way of producing printing plates digitally directly on the printing press, the quality had to be substantially improved. My estimate for designing and building a prototype printing press to conduct a feasibility test of this idea ran from $5 to $8 million. Unfortunately, Howtek was fighting for its life in the litigation over the Pixelmaster at the time and was not in a position to make any risky investments in a new technology prototype, not to mention supporting the project afterward if it worked. Nonetheless I offered this invention at no charge to the Howtek board.

As expected, the board, after much discussion, unanimously and officially declined my offer. I had abstained from voting in the decision, as did my son Larry, who was also on the board. The company just could not make the required investment to develop and manufacture a digital printing press that could produce its own plates directly on the press. I then informed the board that it was my intention to make this very high-risk investment personally through a new company that I would form specifically to design and build this new prototype. Very quickly after that meeting, Larry came to me and said that he wanted to be my partner in this company and was willing to make an investment equal to mine so that he could own half of this new company. At the time he was finishing his MBA, taking day and night classes at New York University. I was thrilled to hear that my son wanted to become a businessman and my partner.

So, in 1986 we started the company and called it Presstek, Inc. I was the chairman of the board, with Larry its president; we each chipped in one million dollars as initial capitalization. We then set out to rent a building where we could assemble a printing press and hire the right people. The person I had in mind for the VP of engineering was Dick Williams, who had remained as the director of engineering at Centronics when the company was sold to Control Data in 1982. Dick was the most creative engineering executive I ever had. When I presented the idea to him, he jumped instantly on board. All told, we were able to attract seven other Centronics employees who we knew were very capable in their jobs. Then, as I always did, I allowed all of them to purchase from the company a limited number of shares of stock at the same price per share that Larry and I had paid. We determined the amount of stock each person was able to buy depending on the importance of the position they held in our company, and if some of the employees didn't have the available funds to pay for their allotted shares, I personally loaned them the amount they needed to make the purchase.

Dick Williams, engineer Frank Pensavecchia, Larry, and I then met for the better part of two days to discuss all the different options for designing and building this prototype. The design and approach to constructing it was entirely the work of our engineering team. We divided the task of building the prototype into three parts. The first included the frame, the power train, and the central cylinder around which the individual printing heads would be mounted. The next task was designing the individual print imaging heads, one each for yellow, magenta, cyan, and, of course, black; these are the negative colors of yellow, red, blue, and black that you end up with when you image the top surface of the printing plate. The third task was to develop a completely new printing plate. We wanted to eliminate the photographic darkrooms, film, and toxic processing chemicals that were a standard part of the color printing industry at the time.

From the beginning we thought that the technology needed to create the image on the printing plate should be done by very small semiconductor thermal lasers. I had done this once before with low-power, low-voltage laser diodes back when we were developing the laser printer. But now we needed high-powered lasers. When we drew up specifications, we calculated that we would need at least 128 individual lasers for each press. We scoured the entire world looking for manufacturers of this type of laser and eventually found one almost in our backyard. The company was called Ensign-Bickford and it was located just outside Hartford, Connecticut.

For more than 100 years, Ensign-Bickford was the largest producer of fuses used to detonate explosives. The fuses were made of gunpowder embedded into what looked like a long piece of rope, but these kinds of fuses were no longer practical for launching the ICBMs and other rockets that the government was developing. So Ensign-Bickford had developed a semiconductor thermal laser that was a kind of electronic fuse. They had just recently completed and equipped the most modern semiconductor laser facility, which could produce four to five times the number of semiconductor laser diodes the U.S. government required. Their huge investment in the development of the product and the overcapacity of their facility was having a detrimental effect on their financial results, since they were a public company.

It just so happened that they were producing a thermal laser very similar to what we required for our printing press, so we contacted an executive at Ensign-Bickford by the name of Tom Dearmin. The company was indeed very interested in the quantity of lasers that we needed. The problem was that they could not sell us the lasers for anything less than $1,240 apiece. But that cost would make our product unsalable, beyond the reach of our customers, because we could not afford to pay more than $400 per laser. So, while using lasers in this technology was desirable, doing so was totally impractical at this time.

Since we still wanted to produce the printing plate on the press itself, we decided to use the spark discharge technology that we had done some work on at Centronics. This technology uses a spark, instead of a laser, to etch holes into the top surface of the plate; the holes then attract the ink onto the imaged portion of the plate. A conductor is needed to attract the spark through the coatings on the plate. Our tests indicated that spark discharge was fast enough and fulfilled the needs of offset printing technology. That took care of the technology.

But we knew that we could not develop a printing press on our own, so we signed a letter of intent with AM International, which was a duplicator company, to help us. We were never capitalized to be a printing press company; we were a technology company, so we always knew we had to do a joint venture with a printing press company to marry the two technologies together. We went public on that basis, and for a year we worked on applying this technology to a new press AM was developing with a common impression cylinder—one gigantic impression cylinder. But AM International proved impossible to deal with and we never completed our contract with them.

That meant we had to cut a deal with someone else. The number one company in the printing press industry was, and still is, Heidelberg. They were even more dominant then than they are today; at the time they had 54 percent of all the installed presses in the world. So we could work with Heidelberg or we had to do a deal with everyone else to get to the same market share. The problem was getting a good introduction to that company. To help us, our printer in New Hampshire, Frank Romano, introduced us to Mike Bruno, a world-renowned printing expert who published an annual volume on the latest technology for the printing industry. Mike was enthusiastic about our innovation and offered to introduce us to Heidelberg. He arranged for us to meet with a man named Rudolf Urig. Heidelberg was, and is still, managed by committee, and Urig reported directly to the board member who was in charge of research and development. This was just the kind of high-level introduction we needed.

But a week before our scheduled meeting, we received a fax saying that Rudolf Urig could not make it. Larry read the fax as saying that a "Dr. Pfizenmaier" would take his place, which left us rather upset. We didn't know how far down the pecking order we had just been handed. When Dick Williams, Larry, and I arrived in Heidelberg, a tall, handsome man in his forties greeted us. We started the meeting at four in the afternoon, skipped dinner, and only ended our discussions at eleven o'clock that night. During the course of this evening we realized just who it was we were talking to.

When we had received the fax, Larry and I had not been impressed that Pfizenmaier was a "Dr." because we assumed that more or less everyone in Germany was a "Dr." But we had read the fax wrong. It wasn't "Dr. Pfizenmaier," it was "Dir. Pfizenmaier"—Director Wolfgang Pfizenmaier. He didn't report to a member of the board who was in charge of research and development; he was that member on the board. We had moved up the pecking order, not down. To this day, I'm convinced that he made the decision to work with us that very night.

The next day, after further meetings, Heidelberg formally agreed to examine our technology in detail and assist us in moving the project forward. A month later, we went back to Germany to do a week of printing with a prototype of our imaging technology using spark discharge and our printing plates, which we would run off on their printing press. We were to make a presentation at the end of the week to the board of directors to see if this project was a "go" or a "no-go." So, we imaged our first set of plates, put it on the press, and they printed beautifully. We were shocked. Dick Williams had learned about color calibration the week before, and Dick thought, this is really good, now we are going to make it better. So he spent the next three days making adjustments but ended up just sucking all the color out of the pages. Rudolf Urig, who became a good friend of the company, just happened to be walking by as Dick was doing the color calibration, and said, "Dick, you've got it reversed." Thus, in the next two days, we had to reprint all the jobs we had misprinted the past three days. But our presentation was a success, and Heidelberg agreed to make a deal with us.

I would spend much of the next year working out a contract with Heidelberg. At one meeting in Heidelberg, Pfizenmaier was insisting on an exclusive. We argued that we could not grant them that without a substantial up-front payment, since we would be unable to do business with anyone else during that period. After a great deal of haggling and trying every kind of approach, Pfizenmaier still would not agree, so I decided to walk out of the meeting. In the elevator down to the first-floor lobby, Larry was both amused and scared, thinking that our deal was dead with the company that produced more than half the printing presses in the world.

But the receptionist in the lobby had received a phone call to stop us and escort us back to the meeting on the top floor. At that point, they agreed to pay us a $3 million engineering fee for ninety days of work, during which we would grant them a ninety-day exclusive, provided that during this period of mutual cooperation we would be negotiating and writing a long-term exclusive contract that included minimum royalty payments to be paid to Presstek for each of the first five years. They also agreed that Heidelberg would use no other technology for at least five years, or two years after we stopped doing business with each other, whichever was longer. That negotiation ploy— walking out when you're not getting what you want—would serve me well in later business deals as well.

The project moved ahead exactly according to plan, and at the end of ninety days, we had the makings of a twenty-year exclusive agreement that had minimal quantities on the number of presses produced each year, with royalty payments of 20 percent of the first sale price of these small presses, which cost half a million dollars apiece.

HEIDELBERG WAS VIEWED as the technology leader in the printing press industry, but they had nothing new, nothing dramatic, to sustain their reputation for the next print show in 1991. This was the ideal time to introduce our technology, but the question was: "How could we get this great technology to market quickly?" We decided that the fastest way would be to adapt our technology to Heidelberg's existing small format press, called the GTO, which was actually bigger than a dining room table. Since the GTO was already in production, we had to retrofit our technology into the existing press. Luckily we were able to engineer our direct imaging system to fit perfectly into the space previously taken up by the water balance units. These components added water to the ink to produce a mixture of ink and water that was fundamental to the chemistry of printing plates, producing the ink-loving and ink-repelling areas of the plates. But our dry offset plates didn't require water. This was a huge and important step forward for the printing industry. In this way, we were able to eliminate a very substantial piece of equipment that required a huge amount of skill to operate.

The new printing press, which we called the GTO-DI—with the DI standing for Direct Imaging—was introduced at Print '91, the largest print show of the year. When you went up the escalator to the show floor, you could turn left for Heidelberg, or right for everyone else; their percentage of the show space represented their share of the marketplace. Within Heidelberg's booth, the largest viewing area was a 250-seat amphitheater. That's where our technology was on display. We had a demonstration every hour for ten days. Hundreds of articles were written about the GTO-DI, and many were rave reviews. It was a real moment in time for the industry. Customers rushed to take delivery on about fifty GTO-DI printing presses during the show.

We managed to get this new printing press into production in less than a year. It was a marvelous achievement. But despite all the interest and the acclaim, and although the press did everything we promised, we realized that the quality of the GTO-DI printed sheet just wasn't good enough. It was probably adequate for the consumer, but it wasn't good enough for the printer. Every printer, even today, will say that they sell the finest quality printing in the world. And because the printer stood between the customer and us, the GTO-DI would never achieve its full potential.

The problem was that the spark discharge technology we used in the printing press was a "tweener"—it was not quite good enough. We needed to introduce the laser printheads. The laser would make our direct imaging technology second to none. But we didn't know if we could acquire the high-powered laser diodes in time to save the company.

Tom Dearmin, the sales engineer we had dealt with at Ensign-Bickford, presented us with a solution that would eventually solve our laser problem. There was a group in Orange

County, California, that was starting a new semiconductor laser company called Opto Power. Tom told us that he was leaving Ensign-Bickford to join this new company as one of the principals and proposed that Opto Power would commit to producing the lasers to our specifications for no more than $400 each, provided of course, we give them a substantial purchase order, which would enable them to finance the project.

We agreed. They made extraordinary progress, and somehow they were able to quickly give us a few samples that permitted us to start our testing. Although Presstek had to subsidize the initial production of these lasers to make it happen, we succeeded in finally breaking the price barrier. Once Opto managed to ramp up the production quantities of our laser, we informed Heidelberg, which immediately realized that these laser printheads would solve the print quality problem. They re-released the GTO-DI with the laser technology and it was very well received. They even promptly replaced the spark discharge systems in all the GTO-DI printing presses they had sold to date with our new laser imaging heads.

Opto Power produced lasers for us for years. In fact, we were the largest nonmilitary users of high-powered laser diodes in the world for five years. Then the telecommunications industry discovered the benefits of high-power laser diodes in their switching equipment, and they began buying up the entire capacity from laser manufacturers. They were moving the pricing up because the demand was so great. So we went from being the biggest buyers of these lasers to bit players. When Opto Power, who was our exclusive supplier, was sold, Tom Dearmin came to work for Presstek as the president of Lasertel, a subsidiary we formed in Tucson to build the lasers for Presstek. We started Lasertel purely as a defensive play. We came within six months of running out of a source of supply.

Presstek still owns Lasertel today. And although it's been a marginal business at best, it's a secured supplier. Without Lasertel, Presstek would have gone out of business.

But the GTO-DI with the laser printhead is not the end of the story, only the beginning of what would prove to be a revolution in the color printing industry. In 1993, Dick, Larry and I, along with Frank Pensavecchia, who is perhaps the finest product engineer I have ever worked with, put together a CAD diagram on large sheets of paper that we taped up to the wall of my apartment on 57th Street. The diagram was of a color printing press we had designed from scratch. This was not a retrofit. Rather, every piece of it was new. We called it the Quickmaster. Compared to the GTO-DI, it was half the cost, half the size, and required much less maintenance and virtually no operator skill.

A prototype of Presstek's Quickmaster, the first short-run full-color printing press, which caused a revolution in the color printing industry

Heidelberg introduced the Quickmaster in 1995 at Drupa, the largest printing equipment exhibition in the world, which now takes place every four years. In the course of two weeks in Düsseldorf, they took orders for nearly 700 Quickmasters, or about one every forty-five minutes. It was the hottest equipment introduction in the history of the printing industry, and there are probably more of these printing presses in the field today than any other printing press in the world. More than 5,000 have been sold in the past dozen years. This success of the Quickmaster is unmatched; it transformed the industry forever.

What we came to understand is that there was much sophistication in the printing industry that required skillful operators, and we were able to overcome all or almost all of the difficulties involved in operating a printing press either through computer software or in the design of the machine itself. The Quickmaster featured a host of innovations. In terms of hardware, there were the laser printheads, of course, the single large central cylinder, and our exclusive printing plates that were surfaced with nonstick silicon, which didn't require water balancing. We also had an automatic plate changer, which would automatically unwind a new plate from a big roll of plates inside the plate cylinder. As each new job began, the new plate would emerge and be placed in the proper position for imaging, always perfectly aligned with the three plates for the other colors. (After use, the plates are then stored back in the plate cylinder until the entire roll is used up.)

There were software innovations as well, which allowed us to electronically adjust the color and the inking of the plates, and then precisely align each color output to produce the final printed sheet without moiré. Previously the press operator had to make this difficult adjustment manually. These innovations sped up the setup of the press, called the make-ready time, to five to ten sheets per job instead of the usual hundred or so it normally took. When you multiply that by eight printing jobs a shift, three shifts a day, over a year's time, you are talking about a substantial saving in time and materials.

This ease of use we were able to introduce into the process led to a very interesting shift in the industry. Half of the Quickmasters were sold to people who had never had a printing press before, because now the only skills needed to operate it were computer skills. Who were the nonprinters buying these printing presses? The service bureaus—the very people who in the past had serviced the printing industry. They had done all the electronic prepress—the typesetting, the photographs, the layout—they essentially would produce the page that would then be made into printing plates and go on the press. These people had never owned printing presses before. Now—because of the low cost of the press, the quick turnaround, the low cost of the printed page, and the minimal skills required—they could.

It's very rare in the history of a business career to create primary demand for a product. Usually what you do is build products that fit into existing markets. Very rarely do you actually create demand that didn't exist prior to the introduction of that product. But that's just what Presstek managed to do.

PRESSTEK OPERATED ON AN OEM MODEL, meaning that we relied on the distribution channel of a large company. It's a brilliant strategy when it works for a small company, and it enabled us to go from zero to a hundred million dollars in four years. And we maintained substantial growth each quarter for five consecutive years with consistent profits of 15 percent after-tax net income. In fact, the reason we were able to do that is that our sales and marketing costs were a fraction of what you would expect because we had the benefit of a worldwide sales force.

By 1995 Presstek was a runaway success. Rumors were rampant about Presstek becoming another Xerox. We were actually being called the "Son of Xerox"! People realized that since each printing press in the field would use at least $10,000 worth of our exclusive disposable printing plates each year, our profits would be enormous. Another rumor held that Xerox was going to purchase Presstek because the Xerox core copier business was under attack by Japanese companies at the time. We did our best to squash these rumors, but our denials had no effect, and our stock price jumped a hundredfold.

But as Heidelberg ramped up production, from 100 units a year, to 150, 200, and 250, by the fifth year, they ended up with an inventory buildup. You never know when you are going to meet the demand of the market. Their excessive inventory problem meant we had a big problem, too. Of course, we always knew that we had a concentration issue, that we had all our eggs in one basket, a basket called Heidelberg. But I had built into our contract with Heidelberg a clause that they couldn't drop the numbers of machines manufactured in any consecutive year by more than 20 percent. That was good in one sense, but it also tended to extend the problem. Instead of one really bad year, it was four years of a thousand small cuts in our sales.

Heidelberg wanted to renegotiate our contract. They had a bone in their throat each time they had to pay us a 20 percent royalty, in addition to the purchase price of our imaging head kit. They found it "unconscionable" that we were making more money on each press than they did. So, they called us to a meeting at Heidelberg headquarters in Germany to discuss a reduction of the 20 percent royalty to 10 percent. When we walked into the conference room on the top floor of the executive building, Larry and I could tell immediately from the grim looks on their faces that something was seriously wrong. Wolfgang Pfizenmaier stood up, greeted us, and then said, "We are here to change our contract in a way that becomes fair to Heidelberg, because this technology for color printing has changed an industry that hasn't changed in fifty years."

After three days of meetings, we finally came to an agreeable conclusion for changes to our master contract. I agreed to a 10 percent royalty, but I had them give up their exclusive. This was important because Heidelberg was actually hindering the growth of Presstek. They had kept us in a niche in the market, which was advantageous to them, but it didn't fulfill the potential of our technology. They kept us in the small printer/duplicator part of the market, when our technology was really ready to move up. But they did not want to encroach upon, or cannibalize, their existing business—they wanted to protect their large press business. Why should they sell a half-million-dollar press to a customer when they could sell them a three-million-dollar press?

That's why we were eventually able to make a deal with Fuji in 1997 to develop an even better printing press with newer technology. The Fuji press utilized a superior impression cylinder, a technology we had acquired when we bought another company, Heath. Though the Fuji press has gone through several iterations in the past decade, more than 200 are sold each year, and it is still the cornerstone of Presstek's business today.

In 1998, I was honored to receive the Rochester Institute of Technology's Cary Award, the most prestigious award in the graphic arts industry, for my several state-of-the-art contributions to the industry. The following year, at the age of seventy-six, I resigned as chairman of the company.

Pressstek was a very significant part of my career. The innovations we introduced were revolutionary. We had developed the world's first direct imaging printing press technology using high-powered semiconductor laser diodes to create images in our unique, chemistry-free printing plates. These technologies have eliminated photographic darkrooms, film, and toxic processing chemicals that had been standard in the color printing industry for decades. Our presses have also reduced the turnaround time for printers and lowered their cost of production. By the end of 2002, more than 90 percent of all the direct imaging digital offset presses installed throughout the world utilized Presstek's direct imaging and plate technologies.

Before Presstek introduced this technology, the short-run color-printing business—5,000 copies or less—didn't exist. Now it's 80 percent of the color printing market. When we first entered the market in the early 1990s, if you wanted to do a color brochure, you had to purchase 10,000 pieces, even if you only wanted a 1,000. The reason is that the cost of printing the first piece was so high, you had to order thousands to bring down the per copy price. Presstek created the short-run color printing business. Even today, once you need more than 300 copies, we can beat any technology—ink-jet, color Xeroxing, whatever—and the quality of our product is the best of all. Traditional lithographic can't match our prices until the 10–15,000 copy mark.

The bottom line is that Presstek still owns the sweetest part of the market today.

··23··

Nineties Interludes

I'M NO BELIEVER IN ASTROLOGY, but other than the runaway success of Presstek, the stars were clearly not in my favor in the mid-1990s. During a period of about three years, I was taken in by a Ponzi scheme, had my identity stolen, replaced my two knees, and was subjected to investigation by the SEC.

The Ponzi scheme began with Zvi Yuz, whom I had met back in 1975 when I had purchased the penthouse apartment at the Cricket Club in Florida. Zvi was a former tank commander in the Israeli army who was selling bathing suits designed and manufactured by a name-brand Israeli company. A fairly good tennis player, he became one of our regular tennis doubles. I played with him every morning I was in Florida during the winter months. Zvi seemed to be doing well financially since, in addition to his bathing suit business, he also ran sports clothing shops in two large hotels.

One day Zvi presented me with an investment deal that he was involved in, called Carmel Foods. He said that if we made an investment in the company, the return on the investment would be 30 percent interest, payable each month. This, he claimed, was very secure, as he personally guaranteed our entire investment, so I decided to have my daughter, Ellen, invest $200,000 from the money that I had in trust for her. She desperately needed regular monthly checks to continue her competitive riding, which she and her husband could not afford. In this way, Ellen would have an additional $5,000 a month taxable income, enough to continue her horse show competitions. For more than a year, I watched Ellen receive her $5,000 each month like clockwork.

I decided it was time to look more carefully into Carmel Foods, as I was considering making a much more substantial investment both for the rest of the family as well as myself. I learned that Zvi owned and ran this company, which was part of a business called Premium Sales Corp., and this in turn was owned and run by a man named Kenneth Thennen. The business involved the trans-shipment of name-brand foods from one part of the country to another and took advantage of a practice common to major food manufacturers, in which they offered to local major supermarket chains special discounts of 10 to 15 percent for the immediate purchase of one to three truckloads of their products when business on those products was slow in their part of the country.

Thennen had worked out a deal with these supermarkets to buy and pay for these discounted truckloads of famous brands like Coca-Cola or Heinz catsup. He would pay the supermarkets a commission of 2 percent for doing the paperwork on this transaction, so the supplier thought that the supermarkets were the local customers. Thennen would then offer the product to supermarket chains in different parts of the country with a 5 percent discount to the purchaser, leaving 3 percent to 8 percent for Premium, whose only costs were the trucking charge, their overhead, and the interest to investors. Since this transaction took less than a week, if they could keep turning the money over, they could afford to pay the 30 percent to their investors and still be very profitable themselves.

Of course, this sounded too good to be true, but when I was told that Merrill Lynch had itself invested $40 million, I decided to do my own due diligence. I visited the office of Carmel Foods and saw about fifty people hustling around on computers and on the phones. I then visited their warehouse, which was a typical one-story building with about ten people working there and an inventory that looked more like a supermarket than a wholesaler's warehouse. They explained to me that they used this space as truck-stop parking when they couldn't immediately deliver the trailer to the customer.

I also had my accountant Harvey Teich come down to Florida and do his own due diligence and examine the books of Carmel Foods. Premium Sales Corp. would not allow Harvey to see their books, but they did show him around their office and warehouse. Premium paid 36 percent directly to Carmel on the invested capital that Zvi was responsible for, which came from his family, friends, and relatives in the United States, as well as those in Israel. Zvi paid everyone 30 percent interest and kept the remaining 6 percent for his own company. Carmel Foods paid to each investor the monthly interest payments on time. After talking to several investors, who had received monthly checks for one to two years without a glitch, I decided to invest $5 million and have all five of our children—mine and Kit's—make whatever investments they could. My accountant likewise invested in the company.

It was wonderful! We all received our checks on time each month, and we all had additional disposable income that allowed us to live a life that we would normally not be able to afford. But no one realized that the interest was being paid from new investor money and not from earnings by the trans-shipping business.

As you might expect, all this was too good to be true and too good to last and came to an end in 1994, when Florida's attorney general charged Premium Foods and Kenneth Thennen with fraud and conducting this business as a Ponzi scheme. Everyone's monthly checks came to an abrupt halt, with a capital loss of the entire amount we had invested. Thennen and his son were arrested, and it took almost a year to find them guilty. The government prosecutors confiscated all of the records and inventory, and the judge appointed an executor to manage what was left in an attempt to recapture any of the assets that could be returned to investors.

The attorney general discovered that many of the suppliers of foodstuffs and other individuals who assisted Premium in deceiving people and who had accepted bribes to help entice new investors were in fact parties to the misrepresentations. Some of these were major companies with substantial assets, while some had insurance policies for such events. Merrill Lynch, by the way, had never been an investor; I had simply been given the phone number of someone who had accepted a bribe to confirm that spurious claim.

As a result my family and I took a tax loss on this investment of more than $7 million. But much to everyone's surprise, about three years after the scheme blew up, all of the investors had their original investment returned minus the accumulated dollar amount of their monthly interest payments. Zvi and his company were cleared of any wrongdoing, but his personal guarantee was worthless, because his entire net worth was invested in this Ponzi scheme. We recovered 80 percent of our investment and went on about our lives.

A large number of Zvi's investors were deeply unhappy with him, so one day, while pulling into the parking garage of a hotel where he owned a sportswear shop, he was assassinated by a bearded man who, security cameras revealed, walked up to

Zvi, pulled out a gun, and shot him in the head. This murder has never been solved and his wife and two children, whom I loved, shortly thereafter moved to Montréal, Canada, where her parents, who also lost a great deal of money in the scheme, were living. This was a very unhappy ending of a decade-long friendship between our two families.

THE STRANGEST EPISODE IN MY LIFE began in 1994 when my office started receiving phone calls from people I did not know, who wanted to speak with Howard Finkelstein. At first we thought these were just wrong numbers, but when we began to ask the callers where they had gotten the number, they said that it either came from the telephone book or from the information operator. Upon further investigation, we found that someone had listed the name of Howard Finkelstein with our office phone number.

We then learned from numerous sources of a rumor circulating that Bob Howard of Presstek was really Howard Finkelstein, a felon convicted of swapping stocks for fur coats and the transportation of women across state lines for immoral purposes. The FBI was supposedly investigating Finkelstein's activities. Then one day I received a phone call from a reporter from the *Wall Street Journal,* who asked me several questions to try to determine if I was, in fact, Howard Finkelstein. Granted, there were a few similarities. For instance, Finkelstein and I had both lived in Bayside, Queens, at one time. But when the reporter told me that Howard Finkelstein had been in jail, I produced my calendar as evidence that I had made a speech at the Presstek annual stockholders meeting, while my passport showed that I had twice traveled to Europe during the time Finkelstein had spent in jail.

In the course of my conversation with the reporter, he told me that the *New York Times* was about to publish an article about my being Howard Finkelstein, and the *Wall Street Journal* didn't want them to get an exclusive on this story. By this point in the conversation, the reporter said he was convinced the rumor wasn't true: I could not be Howard Finkelstein. But this story would not be his.

I immediately called the *New York Times* from my second home in France and asked to speak with the reporter assigned to my story, Susan Antilla, but she was not in the office, so I left my name and number. About an hour later, Antilla called back, informing me that her story was scheduled to run in the newspaper in just forty-eight hours. I suggested that my son Larry call her and arrange for a meeting in my attorney's office in the Chrysler building, where he could present proof that I had never been Howard Finkelstein, alias Bob Howard.

The meeting took place the following morning in my attorney's office where Larry showed her several documents that should have left no question in her mind that I was not Howard Finkelstein. These included the stamps in an expired passport, indicating that I left the country and returned several times during the period that Finkelstein was in prison. Additionally, she was shown my fingerprints taken by the FBI in conjunction with my application for a casino license in the state of Nevada. She was also shown a newspaper article about an interview I had given to the *New York Times* at a meeting of the New York Society of Brokerage Analysts in New York City while Finkelstein was in jail.

After she had seen everything, my attorney then asked her point-blank, "Are you going to publish this article?"

Her reply was a very clear and loud "Yes."

My attorney then said, "Are you interested in the truth or a story?"

As she walked out the door, she responded, "A story."

The article, which ran the next day on the first page of the business section, was totally false and misleading. The reporter actually knew that her story was a fabrication. On the same day the *Times* story appeared, the *Wall Street Journal* ran the story, but they concluded that I was not Bob Howard the swindler and the rumor was not true.

But the following day a small, one-inch retraction was published by the *New York Times*, which read in part: "Mr. Howard's lawyers presented The Times yesterday with documents and other information regarding his identity. After inspecting them, The Times finds no credible evidence to support the rumor. . . . The Times regrets having printed the rumor." The next day the newspaper published a follow-up story by Susan Antilla that was headlined "Presstek Says Rumors Are False."

By that time I was on my way back to New York to be fingerprinted by the FBI, as conclusive proof that I was not Howard Finkelstein. On November 1, an article appeared in the *New York Times* stating that the SEC had concluded that Robert Howard and Howard Finkelstein were "definitely" not the same person. But it was too late; my good name had been tarnished.

This had been such an outrageous attack that six years later, before the statute of limitations ran out, I filed a suit in New Hampshire against Susan Antilla, who was defended by attorneys for the *New York Times*. After three days' deliberations, the jury was out for only two hours and came back with an award of $465,000 in compensatory damages for holding me in what is called "false light," though they rejected my claim of defamation. Unfortunately, their lawyers kept finding reasons to appeal the case. Eventually, I tired of spending a substantial amount of money on legal fees as well as continually having to come back to the United States from my home in France for hearings or meetings with the lawyers. I finally decided to drop the matter and begin enjoying my retirement. The court's ruling in my favor was ultimately overturned for failing to prove actual malice on the reporter's part. There had been a great deal of newspaper coverage about my victory over the *New York Times* in this litigation, and that, in the end, would be my satisfaction.

But the fact is the article did irrevocable damage to my reputation and still nips me in the heels from time to time more than a dozen years later.

TWO YEARS AFTER THE START of the Finkelstein episode, I was the target of an SEC investigation for possible manipulation of Presstek stock, which the *Wall Street Journal* said had "astronomical valuations relative to the rest of the market." At the time, the shares of Presstek were trading about twenty times earnings. Indeed, Presstek stock became a phenomenal performer, rising from less than $25 a share in November of 1995 to a peak of $100 in May of 1996, with those figures adjusted for a subsequent stock split. In addition, the shares of the company had been subject to heavy short selling by speculators whose losses had piled up as they continued to bet on the company's decline. People unfamiliar with the industry doubted that our technology, which allowed color printing without chemicals, was as revolutionary as it has since proven to be. On top of it all, the sales of some of my Presstek stock over the previous year was interpreted as a belief that the stock was overvalued. But what I sold represented but a small portion of the Presstek stock that I owned. Besides, I was seventy-three years old and not in the best of health at the time, and I was selling some stock to leave my survivors with enough cash to pay the inheritance taxes if the need arose.

The following year, however, I agreed to pay $2.7 million in penalties in settlement of a Securities and Exchange Commission suit charging me with making false and misleading statements about Presstek. The SEC suit cited the company's relationship with an analyst for the Pennsylvania Merchant Group, an investment-banking firm that had issued a bullish report on the company's stock after the analyst had submitted it to us for comment in November 1995. After making corrections to the report, Presstek had distributed the analyst's report to investors. I felt that the SEC accusations were unjust as it is common for companies to review an analyst's reports for factual errors and it is common for companies to distribute such reports to interested investors. But in the end I was just pleased to put the matter behind me.

SOME MIGHT SAY THAT THIS EPISODE cut me off at the knees, but the blame for my double-knee operation that took place in 1996 lay not with the SEC but with that snowman episode that had occurred back in 1960 when I dislocated my knee. That injury had given me all kinds of knee and back problems over the years. But the double-knee replacement didn't stop me from conducting business as usual.

During my recovery, from my hospital bed, I made the Delta V acquisition for Presstek. We needed a way of making the imaging plates for our color printing presses, because at the time the company that was making them for us was having quality control problems. Since they were also making special battery materials, they had to break down their machines and clean them before producing our plates. Apparently their cleaning job wasn't always good enough, and as a consequence the plates they produced for us were of inconsistent quality. In our search for a solution, we found a company in Tucson that made a coating machine that was ideal for us; it was three times the size of a dining room table. In negotiating the price for such a machine made to our specifications, I figured out that for about the same amount, about $10 million, I could buy the company—and so I did. Kit's son, Brett, eventually went to work for me at Delta V. We would later sell the company itself, but ever since that purchase Presstek has had a machine that enabled us to make our own plates. Since we are the sole providers of these plates, it has been very much like printing money.

By the end of the decade, my life had taken a turn for the better. In September 1999, I was chosen to receive the Albert Einstein Technology Gold Medal, which is awarded for outstanding technological achievement each year by the Jerusalem Fund of Aish HaTorah. The prime minister of Israel himself would be presenting me with the medal in Israel two months later. The invitation stipulated that this six-day trip was a gala event and that the Israeli government would pay for all expenses. The invitation was just for three additional people, my wife and any two other people of my choosing, but I was allowed to take additional people on the trip if I paid the government's cost per person of $3,800, which I was glad to do. I offered all of my children, grandchildren, and my sister, her daughter, and her son-in-law the opportunity to come to Israel and participate in this significant event and enjoy a memorable vacation together.

Almost everyone came: a total of eighteen people. We all had a first-class nonstop flight on El Al, the official Israeli government airline, from New York to Tel Aviv, where we were warmly greeted on the tarmac by a dozen-member singing group as we stepped off the plane. In the days that followed we visited the Western Wall to see an underground excavation about 75 feet below the base of the Wall where a civilization existed some 3,000 years ago. We also visited the Yad Vashem holocaust memorial, the Jewish open food market, the Masada ruins near the Dead Sea, the shrine that contains the Dead Sea

As part of its fiftieth anniversary celebration in 1997, the United
Nations International School honored me, "the School's most gener-
ous private benefactor," seen here shaking hands with Kofi Annan,
who was then Secretary-General of the United Nations.

Scrolls, and Rachel's Tomb. Helicopters took us to many of the
historic locations in Israel, as well as to Jordan, where we saw
the lost city of Petra, where beautiful structures are carved into
living rock, and had a personal meeting with the King of Jordan's
brother to talk about ways they might attract investments in
their infrastructure that would permit the creation of American
high-tech manufacturing jobs in Jordan. One evening we even
visited a tribe of nomads in their encampment in the desert.
The whole visit was a whirlwind, every moment remarkably
well planned by our hosts.

In 1999, Benjamin Netanyahu, the former and present prime minister of Israel, presented me with the Albert Einstein Technology Gold Medal for outstanding technological achievement.

The last evening we attended a formal dinner where we heard speeches by B. Benjamin, a famous Israeli historian, and Ehud Olmert, the mayor of Jerusalem. Benjamin Netanyahu, the former prime minister, then gave a very moving speech and presented to me the Albert Einstein award with a hug and a kiss, as my entire family looked on. It was a tremendously emotional moment for me.

·· 24 ··

A Company Transformed

WHAT HAPPENED NEXT HAD NOTHING to do with my interest in the female anatomy.

In 2001, foreseeing a decline in the graphic arts and photo finishing industries, Howtek elected to refocus its efforts and transformed itself into a software-oriented company by way of acquisitions, which quickly increased its product offerings for the health-care medical-imaging industry. The following year the company acquired Intelligent Systems Software, Inc., a young, privately owned Florida company whose Computer-Aided Detection (iCAD) MammoReader for breast cancer had been approved by the FDA. In the acquisition, Howtek changed its name to iCAD so that we would be identified as a software company, rather than as a hardware company. Then, in December 2003, iCAD acquired Qualia Computing, Inc., an Ohio company whose CAD system for breast cancer detection had also been approved by the FDA. Almost overnight, the company had undergone a radical transformation.

Early detection of cancer is the key to a better prognosis, and iCAD's software promised to help radiologists identify subtle characteristics that may be associated with various forms of the disease. Using patented algorithms to mark suspicious areas, iCAD's software can identify characteristics that may warrant a second look by the radiologist. Performed as an adjunct to mammography screening, the system can help find 23 percent of cancers an average of fourteen months earlier than traditional screening alone. And since it is reimbursable in the United States under federal and most third-party insurance programs, iCAD's software packages would in just a few years become the gold standard of care in breast cancer detection. But as it was with Howtek for seventeen years, iCAD found itself in financial difficulty in its early years and again I was forced to step in as its only banker.

Still struggling by 2006, iCAD started merger negotiations with a company named R2, which was our only competitor in the field. Until we entered the CAD business, R2 had had a monopoly on breast cancer detection systems. We spent two expensive and disruptive months of negotiation. My main concern was that R2 could, through due diligence, destroy our business, and since I had no regard for their integrity, that was a major concern. At a board meeting to approve the signing of a very complicated contract, I advised the board that this transaction was too dangerous, and that we risked getting basically nothing for our company. So the board unanimously decided to terminate the merger discussions; iCAD would remain an independent company.

What I privately recommended we do instead was get rid of CEO Scott Parr with a fair departure agreement and hire a professional team to manage the company. Since Parr had run the company, we had seen a mass exodus of some very talented people from the two acquisitions that had changed Howtek into iCAD. Parr micromanaged the company: he made all the decisions, even the smallest ones, which is a very destructive way to run a business. His prior experience involved a hostile takeover of a company in financial difficulty, then cutting the legs off the management team that had caused the financial failure. Parr was the kind of person you need if you wish to tear a company down, but it takes an entirely different set of management skills to rebuild a company when you want to merge two acquired management teams into an efficient, single-company operation. So the board fired Parr in July 2006.

I told my son Larry that since I was eighty-three years old at that time and wanting to slow down, and since he was substantially less active in his venture capital business, that he should take over my role as chairman of this company and be responsible for its reorganization and refinancing. Much to my surprise, despite his apparently lackadaisical style, he got the job done brilliantly.

Larry began by locating an executive search firm that charged what I felt was an exorbitant fee, wanting half of the money up front. After he and I spent many hours outlining to these people just what the duties and responsibilities of the chairman should be, as well as having them understand the business that we are in and the future prospects of that business, they presented us with the resumes of about half a dozen very qualified executives. We decided to interview one of them, and after the interview we made an offer to this individual on one condition: that he must move to southern New Hampshire where the company was located. After several weeks of discussions with his wife and children, he decided not to accept our offer because he didn't want to relocate. I felt that living in Pennsylvania and working five days a week in New Hampshire was an unacceptable alternative. In my years of experience I found that such an arrangement is unworkable; the top guy has to be hands-on management, 24/7.

Faced with this dilemma, we had to start looking for a top executive for this struggling company all over again. Fortunately the search firm then introduced us to Kenneth Ferry, who had been the senior vice-president and general manager of the Global Patient Monitoring business of Philips Medical Systems, the market leader in the health-care industry. Ferry had over twenty-five years of prior experience in the health-care technology field, with more than ten years experience in senior management positions. He had such impressive credentials that we gave him an offer he couldn't refuse. He came to work for the company as its president and CEO in May of 2006 and brought with him three other executives who had worked with him for several years. The compensation package that we gave Ken and these three executives was at least double what I had ever offered anyone.

Not only did Larry and the headhunter talk me into going along with these compensation packages, but they had me increase my line of credit to the company as well as invest another $2 million, with an option to convert my stock any time I wished for the current market price. In order to induce me to do something that did not fit into my plan of disengagement, both Larry and Ken agreed to invest an additional $500,000 of their own money on the same basis as my $2 million. Hoping for the best, I agreed to this arrangement. But frankly, I wondered if these people could make a real company out of troubled iCAD.

Shortly after Ken started his restructuring and rebuilding of the company, we canceled the contemplated merger with R2 at the eleventh hour, leaving them in a state of shock. R2's biggest customer was Hologic and our biggest customer was General Electric. These two companies were at each other's throats in a fight for market share of the breast cancer detection equipment business. At that point, Hologic decided to buy R2, which was in far worse financial shape than we had thought. This left iCAD as the only company providing this kind of analytical breast cancer detection software to others. Aside from GE, which dominated this sector of the industry, there were six other companies supplying heath-care equipment worldwide that needed our software for their equipment offerings. The process of getting the FDA to approve new software algorithms such as ours is so long and cumbersome that one by one all of these companies chose instead to include our software as an option in their systems.

That's the situation as it exists today, almost three years after the new management team started at iCAD. To date, the company has placed more than 1,800 of its CAD systems in mammography facilities worldwide, and the company is now developing solutions for use with virtual colonoscopy to improve the detection of colonic polyps. For the first time since its beginning as Howtek in 1984, the company had a positive cash flow and was profitable for the first time in 2008. And after twenty-four years, I was finally paid back the millions I had loaned the company over time. I'm really proud of the management team, the scientists, all of the employees, and, of course, my son Larry, all of whom in their own professional way contributed to what is now the apparent success of a company that had been badly mismanaged for so many years.

· · 25 · ·

Tesla's Death Ray

I WAS LIVING A FAIRY-TALE RETIREMENT in France. I had few responsibilities other than managing my portfolio and my real estate investments in New Hampshire, though I was still chairman of ICAD. In other words I could take care of business with about four hours of work a week. For all practical purposes, 95 percent of the time I could do what I wanted to do instead of what I had to do. So I began writing this book, played a good deal of tennis, and swam a couple of times a day in my indoor pool.

But soon after the turn of the century, I became depressed for the second time in my life. It was probably because I had so little real business to occupy my time. I became irritable, unreasonable, and wanted either to be alone or to sleep much of the time. This continued for about a year, but early in 2002 we received a visit from Kit's son, Brett, who was working at Delta V in Tucson and had run into Tom Dearmin. Tom had been a good friend until his departure from Lasertel on less than friendly terms about three years previously. Brett told me that Tom very much wanted to reestablish contact with me and renew our friendship. He was now a consultant for Raytheon's Directed Energy research group in Tucson, and he had a business proposition to discuss with me.

What Tom wanted to tell me about was a new ultra-short pulse laser discovery that produced a phenomenon called filaments. The military wondered if filaments could be utilized to produce a laser-guided energy weapon. Many people, including a dedicated group at Raytheon, had been working for almost four years trying to understand filaments and learning to control them, but with little or no success. Since I was ready, willing, and eager to get involved in a new business venture, I decided to bury the hatchet with Tom and visit him to discuss filaments with the executives of Raytheon. The meeting would take place about a month later, which gave me plenty of time to read the published papers and other technical descriptions of work that had been performed on filaments up until that time.

Mike Boone, a Raytheon executive, with two engineering scientists, Stephen McCahon and Joe Hayden, headed the Directed Energy program at Raytheon. I met privately with them and Tom on my third day in Tucson. Together we prepared a proposal that Tom would present to the executive board of the Directed Energy group at Raytheon. This proposal was quite straightforward: if Raytheon would contribute to a joint venture that is equally owned and furnished the services of Steve, Joe, and two or three other scientific individuals as required, I would fund the joint venture for any and all other expenses except the compensation for these individuals. We proposed a three-month feasibility study to better understand filaments and to see if there was a way we could learn to control them. We agreed that the two companies would jointly own and have equal rights to any intellectual property that emerged from this venture. At that time I felt that this project would be intriguing and fun since it would take place in Tucson in the winter, which has delightful weather at that time of year.

Our first months of hard, dedicated work produced no tangible results, however. We came to the conclusion that in order to understand filaments we had to design and build a test system that would allow us to evaluate the various combinations of twelve to fifteen complex variables that accrued in the ultra-short billionths of a second that the pulse laser fired. I felt that this was the only way to find the right combination of variables that would permit us to reproduce and control the filaments that a tetra-second laser generated.

My proposal to Raytheon was very simple. If we each contributed $5 million through our joint venture, we might be able to build this unique short pulse laser technology test system. It was a $10 million gamble that I thought would prove worthwhile. But Raytheon rejected the proposal because they said they never invested any of their own money in the development of new technology for government business because it takes at least two to three years to get funding from the government. We then exchanged legal documents to dissolve the joint venture. We gave them copies of every document and experimental test result, together with all of the records we had up to that date, so that they could have no future claim against any further developments we might make.

At that point Tom, Steve, Joe, and I decided that we would start a new company there in Tucson and call it Ionatron. Since they had no money to invest, I would fund the venture and receive 53 percent of the stock of this new company; the others would share the balance, with Tom getting a little more than Steve or Joe. I had never structured any of my twenty-six previous companies this way. It was my intention to have this company be short-lived and fun. I certainly never intended it to become a public company.

It took $8 million of my money and seven months to complete

the design and fabrication of our proprietary Ultra Short Pulse Laser Test Research and Development System. This would permit us to get some helpful results and test our knowledge of filaments: how to create, control, and use them. With the help of, and available time on, a government-owned Raytheon super-computer, we quickly achieved positive results from our new laser system. The ultimate mission of the program was to use an Ultra Fast Pulse Laser with comparatively little power to create what we called a Laser Induced Plasma Channel (LIPC), which is a straight-line conductive channel that could carry very high voltage electrical energy and be used as a destructive force weapon. In short, a death ray.

The death ray had been the dream of Nicola Tesla, the Serbian-American inventor and electrical engineer whose reputation has always been overshadowed by that of Thomas Edison. Tesla had always been a hero in my eyes. He invented the radio, the light bulb, the speedometer, the bladeless turbine, and alternating current (AC) power generation, which is the basis of America's power grid. He licensed his AC induction motor to Westinghouse and they were supposed to pay him 10 percent on every motor sold, but they didn't, and Tesla died penniless in 1943. He had also wanted to control electricity and lightning and had invented the Tesla coil, which creates a high voltage discharge.

I was now trying to achieve what Tesla never could—the control of high voltage electricity. Our model, like Tesla's, was nature. When lightning strikes, it creates a channel through which the lightning actually travels. Likewise, the technology we were developing would create a plasma channel to transmit the high voltage electricity. To create this channel we had to learn how to control the filaments generated when you fire an ultra short pulse laser. Because the filaments start and stop, we had to figure out how to bundle or connect the filaments together in order to create a channel of any length. That way, high voltage electricity fired through the channel could jump from one filament to another continuously. We had to do this because, while the filaments travel at the speed of light, the electrical charge that flows through the channel moves more slowly.

At an Ionatron field test in Arizona, still laser sharp at the age of eighty

All current weapons that use lasers as a destructive force rely upon the power of the photons to heat and destroy the target. The LIPC, on the other hand, only uses the laser to create a conductive channel for the insertion of high voltage energy, which can be controlled to destroy the target. This technological breakthrough could be used in weapons systems for many decades to come. When retired U.S. Navy Rear Admiral Thomas W. Steffens first saw a demonstration of this technology in 2002, he commented: "This will change the nature of warfare and the battlefield long into the future." From that moment on he became one of our most outspoken proponents, and after his second retirement, he became a member of Ionatron's board of directors.

For two years, all went well at Ionatron, until we got caught up in political intrigue between the different branches of our unbelievably inefficient government. Virtually everyone in every branch of government behaves in a manner that exploits and expands his or her job or position without regard to what's best for the country. I found very few exceptions to this process in my weekly visits to Washington during the Ionatron years.

In 2003, just as we were beginning to get some very encouraging results with the LIPC, Ionatron was awarded its first government contract. We received a $10 million order for a transportable demonstration LIPC unit that the Navy wanted to test for stopping small boats from attacking large Navy vessels, as happened in the USS *Cole* incident.

That year we hired the Washington, D.C., office of Blank Rome's government relations group to do our public relations. Several people in their office had special relationships with various influential people, such as Major General Tony L. Corwin, who had three decades of military experience and had recently joined the firm. He had been the legislative assistant to the commandant and director of Legislative Affairs for the United States Marine Corps, a high post in the Pentagon. He was then in charge of making any appointments we needed with the various military departments and individuals. There were layers of individuals involved in every transaction, every conversation, and every technical update, so that everyone would be on the same page as the technical improvements in the program were implemented.

During this process, we had periodic visits from these VIPs to our factory in Tucson, Arizona, especially during the winter when it's very cold in Washington and warm in Tucson. Each time a VIP would come to Tucson, we had to spend a week preparing the demonstration of our LIPC technology. And invariably it did not live up to their expectations. Whenever I was in Tucson, I tried to set rigid time schedules for each phase of technological improvement. We had a very substantial development budget that not only had dollar commitments but hopes and aspirations about technical advancement. We had to put an end to the unfulfilled expectations of our customers time and time again.

Then in 2004 we managed to get a meeting with John Murtha, the chairman of the House Appropriations Defense Subcommittee. Tom had a friend named Fred Way, who had a factory manufacturing high-powered lasers in Congressman Murtha's district in rural Pennsylvania. Fred suggested we hire a lobbyist by the name of Julie Pickering. She quickly managed to get an appointment for us to meet with the congressman. We got a very friendly greeting from Murtha when we arrived at his office a half hour early. When he asked about my background, I mentioned that Milt Shapp and I were partners in a Philadelphia company called Jerrold Electronics very early in my career. It turned out that Milt, who was a two-time governor of Pennsylvania, had been responsible for getting Murtha into politics after Murtha returned from serving in Vietnam.

Murtha spent almost two hours with us, instead of the usual ten to twenty minutes most visitors are granted. He was very interested in knowing about Tom, Ionatron, and me, and the way that we started this business. He then asked us how much money the government had invested in developing this project. I responded: none; I had completely funded the company myself. When he asked how much, I said that I had put in about $8 million so far. He seemed upset about the situation; he thought that since the government was our only customer, the government should be funding it. He then said that he would recommend to his military appropriations subcommittee that Ionatron receive R&D funds to the tune of $8 million "plus up." We were flabbergasted, and from that point on, even though I am a Republican and I disagree with some of Murtha's positions, I have been a staunch supporter and friend of Congressman John Murtha.

In the meantime, Ionatron sought to become a public company. But instead of doing an IPO, Bob Mittman, always more than merely our corporate attorney, convinced me to do a reverse merger. We decided to find a public company that had some cash, no skeletons in the closet, a sufficient number of shareholders, and virtually no business activities, or activities that could be disposed of easily. Mittman had the perfect company for us—US Home & Garden, a failed lawn-care provider that was listed on NASDAQ. USH&G had 2,400 stockholders and nearly $10 million in cash. A reverse merger with them meant that *we* would have 2,400 stockholders and nearly $10 million in cash. The reverse merger, which took place in March 2004, was basically a quick and easy way of going public and getting that highly prized listing on NASDAQ. We then changed the name of their company to Ionatron. Their stock was selling for $.40 to $.50 when the merger took place. I gave the USH&G stockholders about 40 percent of the new company, and of the 60 percent remaining, I kept 53 percent for myself, which meant that I personally ended up with 23 million shares of Ionatron.

In 2004 Ionatron also acquired North Star Power Engineering. We needed expertise that we didn't have for the high voltage

My twenty-eighth company: the family poses as Ionatron joins the NASDAQ on August 17, 2005

portion of the project and I found someone in Albuquerque who was regarded as the guru of high voltage in the industry. He was an engineer, not a businessman, so his company never really made any money. We ended up buying the company for stock. North Star Power Engineering brought to Ionatron an important proprietary understanding of high voltage applications and a portfolio of revolutionary high voltage equipment designs and design concepts.

Meanwhile, Ionatron's sales operation had to deal with the Department of Defense and all five armed services, each of which act independently. It was as though they were at war with one another. I came to realize that the primary task of each service is to protect its own turf and get as much government money as possible. Take, for example, the government funds Congressmen Murtha promised us. He had Congress approve $8 million in R&D for the directed laser project at Ionatron.

The fact that we were doing Top Secret development work added yet another layer of bureaucracy to our operations. We were very limited in terms of what we could reveal about our work. Any disclosures made by any executive of the company first had to be presented to the appropriate government office for prior approval. When we made presentations about our technology, we could only speak in general terms and everything we said was monitored by a government security office. We could release very little information to the public. This, of course, caused an SEC full public disclosure problem, because government business was our only business.

THOUGH IONATRON'S CORE TECHNOLOGY involved laser-induced plasma channels, we stumbled upon another technology that might have more immediate benefits for the military. One day we accidentally exploded a detonating cap with a high voltage current that jumped a gap of about eighteen inches. When I saw this, I thought we might be able to develop a defensive technology that would use a high voltage discharge to detonate roadside bombs. So we got a sandbox, like those in children's playgrounds, and filled it with sand. We then put a probe of high voltage over it, and it jumped down and blew up a detonating cap we had buried under two feet of sand. After seeing a demonstration in the spring of 2005, our Department of Defense customers ordered a dozen prototypes, recognizing that our electrical discharge techniques could be used to neutralize some types of Improvised Explosive Devices (or IEDs), the notorious roadside bombs that had produced more than 70 percent of coalition casualties in the conflicts in Iraq and Afghanistan.

That started our development of a vehicle called a JIN, or Joint IED Neutralizer. The vehicle, which has a metal boom that sticks out of the front of the vehicle, can be operated by remote control from a safe distance. The boom emits high-powered electrical pulses that can set off the detonators in roadside bombs. The Army tested a JIN prototype extensively in 2006, and about 90 percent of the IEDs laid in its path were destroyed. Although a Pentagon's task force determined that the device required further testing before deployment to Iraq, the Marine Corps decided otherwise and sent some modified JIN units to Al Anbar province where the Marines had been deployed since 2004.

But the Marines thought that our remote controlled vehicle was too expensive, so they mounted those electronic booms, our counter IED system, on either side of their heavily armored, land-mine detection vehicles. Today the company is still addressing the challenges of fielding the technology it has developed for use with combat-rugged hardware. More than that, I cannot say.

As THE YEARS PASSED, I found it increasingly difficult to run Ionatron, especially because the tragic events of September 11, 2001, had made traveling so very difficult. So, in 2005, after sixteen very happy years Kit and I sold our villa in France and bought a new apartment on Fifth Avenue, overlooking the Metropolitan Museum of Art and Central Park. We gutted the existing apartment, and with the help of a fabulous architect,

Alex Antoinelli, and a great construction company, Silver Rail, we had a magnificent new apartment built for us.

But our new home in New York made it only marginally easier on me to conduct Ionatron business. My schedule usually meant spending in few days in Washington each week and a few days the following week in Tucson. This schedule would be exhausting for anyone, but it was far worse for me since I was in my early eighties at the time. So after giving the company my all for four years, from its inception in 2002, I finally resigned as an officer and chairman of the board of directors in 2006. With 23 million shares, I was, and still am, the largest shareholder, and for this reason, I stopped having any contact with anyone from the company. I have meticulously adhered to that SEC regulation. It was a difficult decision, and though I sometimes regret not staying long enough to see my technological dream come to fruition, for the third time I found myself once again in retirement. Though it was an agonizing, stressful, and disappointing business, dealing with the government was a new experience for me.

Two years after I left, Ionatron found itself in a pickle that required a change in the company's name. It all happened after an article ran in the *Los Angeles Times,* suggesting that the Army was suffering casualties in Iraq that might have been avoided had they quickly deployed our JIN technology. As a result the company's reputation suffered a severe blow. That's why the company is now known as Applied Energetics.

··26··

Last Hearing

BACK WHEN I WAS SEVENTY-TWO and still living in France, I had purchased my first hearing aid. It was not a pleasant experience and I received the worst possible advice from someone I thought was a professional. I was told to buy a single hearing aid for my right ear. With the hearing aid, I then had better hearing than in my left ear. After using the hearing aid for about two years, I found I then lost a great deal more hearing in my "good" left ear. I later learned that when you have hearing loss and you do not quickly provide yourself with a hearing aid for both ears, you lose the ability to distinguish and focus your attention on the conversation you are interested in understanding.

After that first hearing aid purchase in 1995, I bought about ten other pairs of hearing aids in the decade that followed. Each time, I paid thousands of dollars for what I was told was the newest and best hearing aid that would resolve all the problems I had with my previous devices. But I was never able to overcome the difficulties that I, and most of people with impaired hearing, experience, including background noises that prevent those with hearing aids from hearing the conversations they want to hear. Another common complaint is feedback—usually a very annoying whistling noise—that occurs because the microphone is very close to the speaker unit inside your ear.

Then there's the ordeal of getting fitted with a hearing aid, which involves numerous visits to an audiologist to adjust the response of the amplification system within the hearing aid. Despite the use of some very sophisticated equipment, the technique that audiologists use is basically trial and error. And because of the personal attention required to program your individual hearing aid, the audiologist charges thousands of dollars for hearing aids instead of hundreds of dollars based on their actual cost.

That experience prompted me to start my next business in 2005. I decided to modify Radio Shack's Hearing Assist Device and make it wireless and more user-friendly. I wanted to completely separate the hearing aid itself from the control unit, which could take inputs from the telephone, TV, microphones, etc., and give the user the ability to adjust the frequency response of the hearing aid to their liking on the spot very quickly. During my days at Centronics, I had a very strong personal relationship with the founder of Radio Shack, Charles Tandy, and helped his company get into the personal computer business at a very early stage. But I did not approach Radio Shack for the hearing aid because they do not do the kind of R&D, including chip development work, that was necessary to produce what I felt would be the next generation of hearing aid.

All I needed to do was find a company that could design and build some prototypes, which I thought would be a relatively simple engineering task. Checking the Internet and asking the advice of a number of people in the hearing-aid industry, the name Sonomax, located in Montreal, Canada, kept popping up. When I called the president of the company, Nick Leperle, he suggested that I come to Montreal and show him my product so that he could evaluate the prospects for me.

When I arrived in Montreal aboard a 300 Challenger from FlexJet, of which I had just bought a share to ease my travels, the first order of business was to have Nick sign a nondisclosure agreement. Then, after several hours of discussion, he came up with a recommendation for us: the best company for this project was Gennum, a large company located on the outskirts of Toronto that made all kinds of semiconductor chips. A man named Gora Ganguli ran a small division at Gennum, whose business it was to utilize substantial quantities of the semiconductor chips that Gennum manufactured for the hearing-aid industry. Our product could ultimately use a very substantial quantity of Gennum chips.

We had several meetings with Gora that laid out exactly what our technical needs were, a time schedule for the project, our requirements for 30 prototypes, a commitment for 5,000 to 10,000 pieces to be used for initial field testing, and an estimate for the annual production requirements that would increase to millions per year. We also set an estimated price for the finished product delivered from China: $100 a unit. With this product we were targeting the hearing requirements of about 80 percent of the people needing a hearing aid. This would be the key to our success. Gora, who was both an officer and a director of the Gennum Corporation, signed our agreement after presenting it to his board of directors, and I paid them $100,000 upon signing the contract.

Over the next year and a half Gennum delivered several different models of what we called the RHV, but none satisfied the functional specifications we had both agreed upon at the start of the project. It turned out that Gennum had misrepresented the specifications of their newly developed digital transmitter chip, which they called Falcon. This chip was supposed to eliminate the need for a wire, which the Radio Shack hearing device utilized; transmit the sound in high fidelity to a hearing-aid piece in your ear; and be adjustable by the user from a remote unit.

Unfortunately, the Falcon chip never could do the job that Gennum committed to in our contract and we spent the second year of our contract bickering, blaming, and threatening one another. I decided to simply abandon the project and kiss my $100,000 investment goodbye, as it would have cost more than that to sue them in Canada. So I simply walked away from the deal with Gennum. Unfortunately, by that time, I was already knee-deep in a company called America Hears.

WHEN I FIRST STARTED WORKING with Gennum, Gora had recommended that I meet a man named Henry Smith, who owned a company called America Hears, LLC. The company was located in Bristol, Pa., an easy hour-and-a-half drive from my apartment in New York City. I found Henry Smith to be a very knowledgeable audio engineer whose twenty-year-old, highly regarded company was struggling because it was inadequately financed. I decided that Henry and his company would be essential to the success of my hearing-aid product, the RHV. My plan was to have Gennum supply the product, and to have America Hears distribute and support it.

Henry liked the idea, perhaps because his wife was ill and confined at home and he was concerned about his future income. But I thought his valuation of his company was highly inflated. After much discussion and several appraisals of his company, I agreed to give him $1 million in cash up front and the balance of $2 million over a five-year period without any interest in exchange for an 80 percent interest in the company.

Everyone seemed happy with this arrangement. But not long afterward Gora was fired from Gennum for reasons unknown, and Gennum put the entire division up for sale, including the Falcon chip, together with all of the hearing-aid business that they had spent decades trying to develop. Since Gora had all of the necessary connections to have this product very cheaply manufactured in China, he became the unofficial CEO of America Hears. Two months later Gora resigned, however, because his wife refused to move to Bristol, Pennsylvania, which he had committed to doing prior to being hired. Now Henry and I faced the monumental task of finding a new CEO.

We had heard good things about a man named Delain Wright, who had been the managing director of the Siemens hearing-aid operations in the United Kingdom for a number of years. Upon investigation, I found that he had moved to the Boston area because his family no longer wanted to live in England, and he was now looking for a challenging position in the hearing-aid business. We interviewed him, and both Henry and I had no doubt that he was the right man for the job. Wright became the CEO of the new corporate structure we now called America Hears, Inc.; Henry was the executive vice-president.

Wright was profoundly knowledgeable about the industry and knew almost everyone in all the different companies because of all the years he had spent in the industry. So, during the summer of 2007, which I spent in the Hamptons, I let Wright run the company without any input from me, and unfortunately, none from Henry as well. The business spent a great deal of money without any results. Wright, meanwhile, apparently thought that he had unlimited funds available to him. When the summer ended, I quickly saw what he was doing, the people he was hiring, the corporate commitments he was making, and his total lack of understanding of the absolute need for the company to make at least one of the Big Deals he always talked about but never delivered. What he did know how to do was spend a huge amount of money on lodging and entertainment, including $10,000 a month for a furnished apartment in Bristol, Pennsylvania, instead of $65 a night for a nearby motel room for the eight to ten nights a month that he stayed there. He had committed to move his family to Bristol within four months of his employment, but never did so. From the moment he was hired I don't think he spent ten cents of his own money; the company paid for everything, even his chewing gum.

Stepping back to evaluate all the business and personal aspects of this situation, I decided to fire Wright and his friends, and give back to Henry the 80 percent of the company that I owned. I also gave him the $500,000 that Wright had squandered, plus an additional $1,000,000 so that the company had enough working capital, and I let Henry keep the payment that he received when I bought 80 percent of the company. While that arrangement cost me, all told, about $2,500,000, I could afford it. I had made a lot of money in business and Henry was just too nice a man to simply abandon. I didn't want him to get hurt.

I guess that at age eighty-five my killer instincts as a businessman had finally deserted me. I was just too old and did not have the passion to make it all happen. And for the fourth and final time in my life, I retired. Six-plus decades of work should be enough for anyone. Even me.

Epilogue

RETIREMENT IS SOMETHING that most working men look forward to, but so far it hasn't worked for me. It's been more than forty years since I retired for the first time, and a year since I retired for the fourth and "final" time. It's not that I've run out of ideas—location-enabled golf balls, anyone? But projects on that scale may require more time and energy than I have left in me at this point. You never know, though. Throughout my life, great new ideas have energized me as nothing else can.

With free time again on my hands, I was finally able to return to, and finish, the book I began writing at the end of the twentieth century at my villa in the south of France. Only this time I worked from my computer in my newly purchased home in the Wainscot township of the Hamptons. It is a magnificent, two-year-old, five-bedroom house on two acres. Its exterior walls consist principally of glass doors opening onto a terrace and a beautiful, football-field-size backyard, which makes it very easy to live in, and entertain comfortably both indoors or outdoors. A newly constructed indoor pool permits me to swim all year round, a very important activity for me at this age.

This book has taken my full time and effort for the past year. Any errors in my story are unintentional, and hopefully forgivable, as I have relied largely on my memory, except for a few news clippings about my companies and inventions that I managed to save over the years, and the invaluable help of my remarkable sister, Sylvia, who has better recall of some details of my childhood than I do. Today, at the age of eighty-nine, she still promptly goes to work every day at 9:30 a.m. to her office at the United Nations. She has had an outstanding and fascinating career as Special Representative to every Secretary-General of the United Nations since 1962. I am, and always have been, very proud of her.

Telling this story of my life has been a real challenge and a great exercise, pushing the bar of my memory in my twilight years. I hope you have enjoyed learning a little bit about how all those little inventions that I was responsible for—and that may play a part in your lives—came about as my life unfolded.

Since I have not yet completed the cycle of my life, when I will end up in the "bottom drawer" six feet underground, I recently took up bird-watching in the hopes of quelling my restlessness. But frankly, I find the burning desire within me do something and be productive undiminished. I have thought about writing another book, a sexy Las Vegas tell-all, but I'm even more tempted to restart the hearing project with Gora Ganguli. My hearing problem is severe, and I believe I now have the technical solution in hand, a newly developed wireless transmitting device that was the missing piece of technology that ultimately caused the failure of my hearing project two years ago. This project and the millions affected by hearing loss need me—and I need it.

Ironically, the call I am hearing needs no ears.

Acknowledgments

I wish to express my thanks to the following people who materially contributed to my business success that made this book a story worth telling:

- Isaac Greenspoon, my grandfather and mentor;
- Varian Brothers, who started my engineering career;
- Ed Dennis, George Gross, and Larry Morton, who were my first major customers;
- Arthur Coller, Esq., who taught me business smarts;
- Uncle Riley, who was like a father to me;
- Milton Shapp, my first partner;
- Dr. An Wang, a scientific genius;
- Prentice Robinson, an engineering administrator;
- Dr. Murray Fuhrman, who saved my skin more than once;
- Wolfgang Pfizenmaier, the engineering visionary at Heidelberg;
- Frank Romano, who assisted in the development of Presstek's technology;
- Richard Williams, Frank Pensavecchia, engineering masters;
- Robert Mittman, Esq., who kept me out of trouble;
- John Murtha, a believer and supporter;
- and to Patrick Huyghe, Charles DeFanti, Marilyn Garcia, Mara Lurie, Steven Berry, and John Weber, without whose help this book could not have been published.

But most of all, I wish to thank my departed friend Dick Williams, who worked with me on a daily basis for more than twenty-five years. His engineering genius turned many of my visions into successful products and companies.

Appendix 1

Principal Businesses of Robert Howard (1947–2008)

1947 Howard Television, Inc.
Queens, NY
> Assembled television sets using a rectangular TV tube developed at Sylvania Electric Corp. and other commercial TV tubes when the rectangular tubes ran out. Howard gave the company to employees in 1953.

1948 Custom Built Television Corp.
Queens, NY
> The first retail store to sell Howard Television sets. Two additional retail stores added later. The corporation was dissolved in 1953.

1948 Legion Cabinet Corp.
Queens, NY
> The company manufactured all kinds of cabinets, including those for the television sets of Howard Television and Allen B. DuMont. The company was sold in 1953.

1948 Video Products Corp.
Brooklyn, NY
> Manufactured the RCA 630 chassis for use in custom designed television sets. The company was sold for assets in 1953.

1949 Electronics Installation Corp.
Queens, NY
> Installed MATV (Master Antenna TV) and CATV (Cable Antenna TV) systems. The company was sold to Teleprompter in the 1960s.

1950 Jerrold Electronics (joint venture)
Philadelphia, PA
> Developed what would become the largest cable television equipment manufacturer and performed cable system installations. The joint venture with Milt Shapp was dissolved in 1951.

1952 Windsor Cable Corp.
Queens, NY
> A master antenna and cable television system operating company. Sold to Teleprompter in the 1960s.

1953 Gyro Electronics, Inc.
Queens, NY
> Manufactured master antenna and cable television equipment. Sold to Teleprompter in the 1960s.

1955 Polar Distributors, Inc.
Queens, NY
> A distributor for the first through-the-wall air conditioners made by the Lewyt Corp. Later acquired Lewyt's air conditioning division. Polar is operated today by Howard's oldest son, Richard Howard.

1958 Amplitell, Inc. (acquired)
New York, NY

> A television antenna system company acquired by Gyro Electronics. Sold to Teleprompter in the 1960s.

1958 Acme TV Systems Corp. (acquired)
New York, NY and NJ

> A New Jersey and New York cable system company acquired by Gyro Electronics. Sold to Teleprompter in the 1960s.

1958 Jalson Construction Corp.
Melbourne, FL

> A venture that developed a square mile of land and constructed some 1,400 houses in Melbourne, Florida. Sold to a Washington, D.C., developer in 1960.

1959 Municipal Sewer & Water Corp.
Melbourne, FL

> A venture for the development of sewer and water facilities for new subdivisions in Florida. Sold to a Washington, D.C., developer in 1960.

1959 Riverview Construction Corp.
Miami, FL

> A joint venture for building housing in central Florida for members of a national union of government employees. Option contract abandoned.

1960 Audio Matrix Corp.

Bronx, NY

In partnership with Milt Gelfand, developed and produced the "The Boomer," an extruder of plastic for the manufacturing of high quality stereo phonograph records. Sold to RCA Record Corp. in 1961.

1962 Cool Heat Corp.

Long Island, NY

Manufactured a central heating and cooling unit for apartments that gave tenants individual room temperature control. Sold to Weil-McLain in 1964.

1962 New York City Cable Corp.

New York, NY

The original NYC cable television franchise in a joint venture with Howard Hughes Interests, who financed the infrastructure investment. Sold to Teleprompter in the 1960s.

1964 Teleprompter Corp. (major stockholder)

New York, NY

Merged all of Bob Howard's master antenna and cable system operations into one business that was listed on the American Stock Exchange. Sold stocks in 1969.

1964 Wang Laboratories, Inc. (joint venture) (major stockholder)

Tewksbury, MA

A digital computer joint venture with Dr. An Wang; jointly started Centronics for the development of the casino computer system. Stock sold over a 12-year period.

1965 Howro Realty Corp.

Queens, NY

A company formed for real estate and tax shelter investments in the New York area. Ongoing.

1966 Brentwood Yarn Mills, Inc.

Brentwood, Long Island, NY

Novelty yarns manufacturing. Business dissolved and building sold four years later.

1967 Bonanza Hotel & Casino, Inc. (stockholder)

Las Vegas, NV

A 2.5 percent investment in the Bonanza. Subsequently rescued the Bonanza with a loan and was put in charge of selling it. Eventually sold the land to Kirk Kerkorian for the MGM Grand Hotel and Casino.

1968 Centronics Data Computer Corp.

Hudson, NH

Developed, leased, and installed casino control systems before growing into one of the world's leading printer companies with the dot matrix printer. Centronics grew from 7 employees to more than 6,000 with operations and subsidiaries in 27 countries. Sold to Control Data Corp. in 1982.

1973 Gamex Industries, Inc.

Las Vegas, NV

Developed the first electronic slot machine as a subsidiary of Centronics. When Centronics became a printer company, the gaming operations of Centronics were merged into Gamex Industries, Inc. Sold in 1977.

1981 RH Research, Inc.

New York, NY

A personal venture/capital investment activity to prove or disprove the practicality of various inventions. Ongoing.

1984 Howtek, Inc./iCAD

Hudson, NH

Began as a scanner supplier for the graphic arts industry, the company transitioned to a computer aided design (CAD) breast cancer detection system and medical digital scanner manufacturer named iCAD in 2001. Howard resigned as chairman in March 2008.

1986 Presstek, Inc.

Hudson, NH

Developed a rapid four-color printing press system that revolutionized the graphic arts industry. Howard resigned as chairman in 1999. His youngest son, Larry Howard, is still on the board of directors.

2002 Ionatron, Inc. (name changed to Applied Energetics, Inc. in 2007)

Tucson, AZ

Developed and created new technology for nonlethal or lethal weapons systems. Howard started the company in 2001 and resigned as chairman in 2006.

2007 America Hears, Inc.

Bristol, PA

Acquired hearing aids company intended to be the distributor of the RHV hearing device being developed.

Appendix 2

Principal Inventions and Concepts of Robert Howard

1942   Oscillation/movement of the X-ray Buckeye Grid

1944   Low-cost microwave oscillator tube

1944   First accelerometer vacuum tube

1945   Mousetrap filament for proximity fuze for antiaircraft shell

1946   Planar grid triode high frequency oscillator vacuum tube

1947   Designed a 30-inch tube television set (using an RCA patent) with a prototype Sylvania rectangular picture tube, for personal use

1948   Started first company, Howard TV

1950   First cable television line amplifier (single channel) (with Milt Shapp)

1952   First inductive standing wave amplifier (non-electronic)

1952   A radio-transmitted apartment building monitoring system, using an 8-track continuous loop tape recording system, part of an all-electronic Apartment Building Communication System

1956   First transistor TV line amplifier (with An Wang)

1960   Color Photo Negative Analyzer

1961	Design of the first retransmission of TV channels with frequency charger for MATV (Master Antenna Television) systems television application
1961	First extruder (Audiomatic Boomer) for the manufacturing of high-quality stereo phonograph records
1967	A very early digital computer for unlimited multiple terminals online real time (with An Wang)
1968	First casino computer control system for the Nevada Gaming Commission
1969	First automatic casino chip scanner/counter
1970	First dot matrix printer
1970	Centronics interface (with An Wang)
1971	First "electronic" slot machine
1974	First multiple pass color matrix printer
1974	First desktop semiconductor laser printer (with Cannon)
1984	First rotary hot-melt piezo crystal color printer
1986	First desktop high-resolution color scanner
1988	First totally automatic four-color lithographic printing press with on-press imaging (idea)
1989	First on-process thermal imaging printing plate
1989	First on-process thermal digital imaging system
2002	LIPC (Laser Induced Plasma Channel)
2007	RHV wireless/remote microphone hearing aid

Index